It's Elementary!

INVESTIGATING THE CHEMICAL WORLD

Douglas Hayward
Gordon S. Bates
Illustrations by Nyla Sunga

Pacific Educational Press

Vancouver Canada

© 1994 Do-It-Yourself Chemistry, University of British Columbia
ISBN 0-88865-088-4

Published by Pacific Educational Press
Faculty of Education
University of British Columbia
Vancouver, Canada V6T 1Z4
Telephone (604) 822-5385; fax (604) 822-6603

The publisher gratefully acknowledges the assistance of Heritage Canada
and the Canada Council for their assistance with its publishing program.

Canadian Cataloguing in Publication
Hayward, Douglas, 1919-
    It's elementary

    ISBN 0-88865-088-4

    1. Chemistry--Juvenile literature.   I. Bates, Gordon Steven.
II. Sunga, Nyla.   III. Title.
QD35.H39   1944   j540   C94-910646-1

Editor: Janis Barr
Design: Warren Clark
Illustrations: Nyla Sunga
Printed and bound in Canada

10 9 8 7 6 5 4 3 2 1

CONTENTS

To my grandchildren
Alastair David Chaplin and
Leslie Ann Chaplin
—*Douglas Hayward*

To my children Elisa Marie
and Janine Christina
—*Gordon S. Bates*

FOREWORD

For many years university science faculty have lamented young people's lack of interest in science. In 1986, Douglas Hayward and Gordon Bates decided to do something about it. They knew that the key feature that makes science different from other subjects is the experimental method. They also recognized that experiments stimulate young minds and attract young people to science. Douglas Hayward and Gordon Bates wanted to illustrate how challenging ideas and thought-provoking questions can be generated from everyday experiences and observations. Thus the idea to do something to bring the science of chemistry and the experimental method into the classroom was born.

Believing that for their efforts to be successful, young minds had to be intrigued at an early age, Gordon and Douglas directed their efforts towards elementary school students. Douglas has been the team member in the classroom, and from the outset, Gordon coordinated the program and was responsible for fundraising so there were never any direct costs to any of the schools Douglas visited.

Douglas has continued to reach out beyond the school system and has written many articles about chemistry and other areas of science which have been published in several community newspapers in British Columbia. These articles were the beginning of this book. Many of them have now been brought together in what we hope you will find to be an enjoyable introduction to chemistry.

Larry Weiler,
Head (1982-90),
Department of Chemistry, University
of British Columbia

TO PARENTS AND TEACHERS

The best way to understand and appreciate science is to do it just like scientists do. Scientists study the world by asking questions and doing experiments to answer them. Chemistry is the science of matter and matter is anything that has size and weight. Chemists are scientists who ask questions about matter and do experiments with matter to find the answers to their questions.

This book is an extension of our classroom-based introduction to chemistry for elementary school students that was begun in British Columbia, Canada in 1986. *It's Elementary!* continues this hands-on introduction to science and to chemistry in particular.

The experiments in this book are fun, interesting, and safe for children ten to thirteen years of age to do in their own homes or classrooms. All of the equipment and materials required for the experiments can be found at home or at the supermarket. These materials may be used with confidence and are readily available, low in cost, and have been screened for safety by experts.

To further your child's interest in chemistry and science, we suggest that you contact, through your school principal, organizations such as the "Scientists and Innovators in the Schools" program, or a university or college chemistry department in your area to arrange for a chemist to visit your child's classroom. The "Scientists and Innovators in the Schools" program was set up by the British Columbia provincial government, modelled on the authors' "Do-It-Yourself Chemistry" program. Similar programs are in place elsewhere, and there are many individual chemists who are eager to bring the excitement of chemistry to our children.

Together we can help students enjoy science and prepare for the future.

Douglas Hayward and
Gordon S. Bates

EVERYTHING IS CHEMISTRY

This book is an introduction to some of the ideas people have about chemistry. It is about the idea of the simple (the elements) combining to the form the complex (compounds); it is about changes in the form of materials; and it is about all of the things around us. Chemistry and chemicals are everything that we see, touch, eat, breathe, use, and are. Chemistry is not to be feared as something bad or hard to do or to learn—it is something that is fun!

We hope this book will open your eyes to the wonder of one of the most important sciences, and that you will go on to learn and understand more about the world around you.

Born in the Stars

Atoms born in the stars are the building blocks of the universe. The idea that everything in the world is made from atoms started with the Greek philosopher Democritus, 2,500 years ago. Atoms are made of smaller particles called protons, electrons, and neutrons. Each different kind of atom is called a chemical element. You can't break an atom down into smaller pieces and still have the same element. So an atom is the smallest piece of matter that can still be that element. There are 109 elements known today. Of these, 94 occur naturally, and 15 have been made artificially by scientists. Elements and combinations of elements make up all the many different things, both living and non-living, that we see around us.

THE BIG BANG

The universe was formed about 15 billion years ago in a huge explosion called the Big Bang. Many scientists believe that before the Big Bang, everything was contained in one single mass that was incredibly dense. The energy from the Big Bang was converted into hydrogen atoms (atomic number 1) and helium atoms (atomic number 2). In the darkness, these atoms were attracted to each other by gravity, and they collapsed together to form stars. The stars are the source of all the other natural chemical elements in the universe.

The pressure of gravity and the very high temperatures in the centres of stars squeeze the hydrogen and helium atoms together until they melt (fuse) together to form the atoms of the other elements. Chemical elements are constantly being made by fusion from hydrogen and helium in our sun and all the other stars. But this doesn't happen all at once. As stars age and use up their hydrogen fuel, they eventually begin to fuse other atoms together to produce heavier elements like carbon (atomic number 6), oxygen (atomic number 8), and other elements up to iron (atomic number 26).

Most stars eventually explode as novas, sending all of their elements into space to be collected again by gravity and reworked into new stars. Very massive stars will explode with even greater energy to form supernovas. The energy in such an explosion is so great that heavier elements like silver (atomic number 47), gold (atomic number 79), and all the other elements up to atomic number 94 are formed.

About 1% of the hydrogen and helium atoms in the universe have been converted into the other 92 natural elements. About 73% of the atoms in our own sun are hydrogen, and every second, about 600 tonnes (tons) of hydrogen atoms are converted into helium. The energy released in this process is what makes the stars so hot. Enormous amounts of this energy are given off as starlight.

Scientists can identify the elements in the stars because each element emits light when it is heated. You can see yellow light from sodium in fog lamps, blue light from mercury in street lights, and red light from neon in some advertising signs. The other colours in signs are from other gases. An instrument called a spectrometer is used to study the light from the stars and separate it into colours. The colours are spread out in much the same way that water droplets can separate white light to form a rainbow. The different colours appear as a pattern called a spectrum. Each element produces only certain colours, so each element has its own spectrum, just as each person has different fingerprints. The element helium was first identified in the sun using a spectrometer, but then because scientists knew what to look for, it was found on earth.

CHEMICAL AGE

To illustrate the long history of the chemical elements, ask two friends to stand on either side of you. Spread out your arms, fingertip to fingertip, and imagine that each of your forearms, upper arms, and body widths represents one billion years (a thousand million years). This means each of you is five billion years, and together total 15 billion years, the age of the universe. Looking from the back, your friend to the left is A, you are B, and your friend to the right is C. At A's left is the Big Bang when the universe began, and at C's right is tomorrow.

Stars usually last about 3 to 5 billion years. Two or three generations of stars had to build up, live, and die to create enough of the elements to make up the earth. Some elements from these stars were attracted to each other by gravity. As the mass of elements grew larger, it attracted more material, until the earth was formed 4.55 billion years ago. This date is represented by C's left forearm.

Oxygen and hydrogen atoms later combined to form water molecules and filled the earth's oceans. Life appeared as one-celled bacteria 3.6 billion years ago on C's left upper arm. In 3 billion years, they produced the oxygen of the air. Multicelled organisms then appeared on C's right forearm. At the second joint of C's right middle finger, they became dinosaurs. These animals evolved into birds and mammals by the first joint of this middle finger. People and all their history are just on the tip of C's middle fingernail.

Did you know that we are mostly carbon, hydrogen, oxygen, and nitrogen atoms? Although we are only worth a few cents as elements, we can think of ourselves as being made of stardust since every chemical element in our bodies and in everything else around us came from the stars.

SUPERNOVA

On February 23, 1987, Ian Shelton of the University of Toronto was in Chile taking photographs of stars with a telescope. In his pictures, he noticed what seemed to be a bright star that had never been seen before. The star was so bright that he could see it without a telescope. He had discovered an exploding star that has been named Supernova 1987A. Astronomers all over the world studied Supernova 1987A with telescopes, and with instruments carried on planes, rockets, and balloons.

Before it exploded, Supernova 1987A was a blue star called SK-69/202 by astronomers. This star was located outside our own galaxy and could only be seen from the southern hemisphere. It was about 50 times larger than our sun and was formed about 11 million years ago.

After 10 million years, the star ran out of hydrogen and became smaller and hotter. When it reached 190 million degrees, more elements were made through fusion. This gave off so much energy that the temperature of the star kept rising. At a temperature of about 3 billion degrees, the blue star exploded. The explosion created still heavier chemical elements and gave off so much light that Ian Shelton was able to see it even though the light had been travelling in space at a very high speed for 160,000 years before reaching the earth. Supernova 1987A was the first

exploding star in 380 years that was bright enough to see with the naked eye.

Astronomers can predict the ultimate fate of stars based on their mass. Only some stars will become supernovas, and our sun is not one of these. It will eventually explode as a nova, and the outer reaches of

the sun will engulf the earth. But we don't have to worry about it exploding as it will continue to light and heat the earth for several billion years to come.

METEORS

Asteroids and comets orbit the sun just like the planets do. Sometimes comets break apart, but the resulting pieces of ice and rock continue to orbit the sun. These small fragments are called meteors.

Meteors go around the sun in swarms. Each year the earth passes through the swarms, and some of the meteors enter the atmosphere, making showers of meteors. On clear nights you can see meteor showers around the following dates: January 3, April 21, May 4, July 29, August 21, October 22, November 1, November 17, and December 12.

Watch for these meteor showers in the late evening as far away from any light that you can get. You could set up a lawn chair in your back yard away from the lights, and organize a sleeping bag, pencil, paper, and maybe a hot drink. Try to count the number of meteors you see and note where in the sky you see them. What direction are they travelling?

When meteors enter earth's atmosphere from space, the friction made by their path through the air makes even the smallest, dust-sized meteors so hot

they catch fire and burn up. When people say they have seen falling stars, they have really seen the streaks of light made by fast-moving burning meteors as they enter earth's atmosphere from space.

Still, about a thousand tonnes (tons) of meteors survive the passage through the atmosphere and land on the earth every day. After they fall to earth, they are called meteorites. More than 14,000 meteorites have been found so far, most of them on glaciers in Antarctica. Around 700 meteorites have been found in Canada since 1900. In June 1994, Stéphane Forcier found a meteorite about the size of a grapefruit on his father's farm in Québec.

Most meteorites are very tiny by the time they have burned their way through the atmosphere, but some are very large. The largest ever found weighs 66 tonnes (tons)

and landed in Namibia, Africa. In only a few cases have people actually witnessed meteorites landing on the earth.

When very large meteorites hit the earth, they make a bowl-shaped hole called a crater. The largest crater is near Hudson's Bay. It is 640 kilometres (400 miles) in diameter. Other craters are a Canadian arctic crater on Devon Island with a 20 km (12.5 mi) diameter and a crater in Arizona in the United States that is 1.3 km (0.8 mi) in diameter.

Since meteorites have not been changed by weather, volcanic action, or pollution since they were created billions of years ago, chemists can learn about the formation of the solar system from them. Many meteorites are made of iron and nickel, and carbon has been found in some meteorites as

tiny diamonds. Some stony meteorites contain simple compounds that could not have come from plants or animals on the earth. Some materials on earth such as helium are so light that they can escape from the atmosphere. But meteorites are the only source of new material added to the earth.

Earth is not the only body in the solar system that is struck by meteors. The moon is pockmarked with meteorite craters. In July 1994, a spectacular collision of meteors occurred with the planet Jupiter. These meteors were as big as mountains. Virtually every telescope on earth was trained on Jupiter, because such an event has never before been visible to human beings.

THE PERIODIC TABLE

We now know that there are 94 natural elements. But in 1869, only 63 chemical elements were known. A Russian chemist named Dmitri Mendeleev arranged them in rows and columns according to their atomic weight, bringing together elements that were similar to each other. When the table was finished, there were gaps where elements should have been. Mendeleev thought that the gaps could be filled, and he predicted the kinds of elements that should be present but had not yet been found. Chemists searched until all the remaining natural chemical elements had been discovered.

The atomic number of an element is the number of protons in its nucleus. For example, the metal lithium (atomic number 3) has 3 protons. The Periodic Table lists the elements from atomic number 1 (hydrogen) to atomic number 94 (plutonium) in 7 rows, with similar elements in each row arranged in 18 columns. This arrangement organizes certain groups of elements together and makes the Periodic Table a useful tool for predicting which elements will combine with each other.

Chemists have made 15 different kinds of synthetic atoms that do not exist in nature. These elements have atomic numbers 95 to 109. Chemists know from the atomic number of the known elements that any new ones discovered or made must fit into row 7 of the Periodic Table after element 109.

How do chemists make new elements? Elements with atomic numbers 84 to 94 are radioactive, that is, they break up into sub-atomic particles (smaller than atoms) all by themselves. The sub-atomic particles can be used to break up other atoms or to make new atoms in a device called a particle accelerator. The synthetic elements, which have atomic numbers from 95 to 109, are also radioactive. When sub-atomic particles strike target atoms at just the right speed, they combine with them to create new atoms. If the speed is too slow, the particles do not fuse together; if the speed is too high, the atoms are knocked apart. Chemists separate the new atoms from the old ones and study them to learn how they can be used.

The Periodic Table is a shopping list for everything in the universe, living and non-living, including ourselves, the planets, moons, comets, and stars. Living things are made mainly from the elements carbon, hydrogen, oxygen, nitrogen, sulphur, and phosphorus from the right side of the Periodic Table. Metal elements from the left side are also needed in small quantities in all living things. Examples are iron in our blood to carry oxygen and magnesium in plants to absorb sunlight.

The Periodic Table allows chemists to plan how to make new substances and invent new ways of using the substances we already have.

hmm... perhaps a bit more..... ... phosphorus!

Br

SALE!

SPECIAL!

PERIODIC TABLE OF THE ELEMENTS

Legend / Key

- Atomic Number → 6
- Element Symbol → C
- Relative Atomic Mass (1985 IUPAC) → 12.011
  - *for the radioactive elements the mass of an important isotope
- Element Name → Carbon

- Fe Solid element
- Br Liquid element (20°C)
- Ar Gaseous element
- Es* Artificial radioactive element

Main Table

1	2	3	4	5	6	7	8	9	10	11	12	13	14	15	16	17	18
1 H 1.00794 Hydrogen																	2 He 4.002602 Helium
3 Li 6.941 Lithium	4 Be 9.012182 Beryllium											5 B 10.811 Boron	6 C 12.011 Carbon	7 N 14.00674 Nitrogen	8 O 15.9994 Oxygen	9 F 18.9984032 Fluorine	10 Ne 20.1797 Neon
11 Na 22.989768 Sodium	12 Mg 24.3050 Magnesium											13 Al 26.981539 Aluminum	14 Si 28.0855 Silicon	15 P 30.973762 Phosphorus	16 S 32.066 Sulphur	17 Cl 35.4527 Chlorine	18 Ar 39.948 Argon
19 K 39.0983 Potassium	20 Ca 40.078 Calcium	21 Sc 44.955910 Scandium	22 Ti 47.88 Titanium	23 V 50.9415 Vanadium	24 Cr 51.9961 Chromium	25 Mn 54.93805 Manganese	26 Fe 55.847 Iron	27 Co 58.93320 Cobalt	28 Ni 58.69 Nickel	29 Cu 63.546 Copper	30 Zn 65.39 Zinc	31 Ga 69.723 Gallium	32 Ge 72.61 Germanium	33 As 74.92159 Arsenic	34 Se 78.96 Selenium	35 Br 79.904 Bromine	36 Kr 83.80 Krypton
37 Rb 85.4678 Rubidium	38 Sr 87.62 Strontium	39 Y 88.90585 Yttrium	40 Zr 91.224 Zirconium	41 Nb 92.90638 Niobium	42 Mo 95.94 Molybdenum	43 Tc 98.9063* Technetium	44 Ru 101.07 Ruthenium	45 Rh 102.90550 Rhodium	46 Pd 106.42 Palladium	47 Ag 107.8682 Silver	48 Cd 112.411 Cadmium	49 In 114.82 Indium	50 Sn 118.710 Tin	51 Sb 121.75 Antimony	52 Te 127.60 Tellurium	53 I 126.90447 Iodine	54 Xe 131.29 Xenon
55 Cs 132.90543 Cesium	56 Ba 137.327 Barium	La-Lu 57 to 71 Lanthanides	72 Hf 178.49 Hafnium	73 Ta 180.9479 Tantalum	74 W 183.85 Tungsten	75 Re 186.207 Rhenium	76 Os 190.2 Osmium	77 Ir 192.22 Iridium	78 Pt 195.08 Platinum	79 Au 196.96654 Gold	80 Hg 200.59 Mercury	81 Tl 204.3833 Thallium	82 Pb 207.2 Lead	83 Bi 208.98037 Bismuth	84 Po 208.9824* Polonium	85 At 209.9871* Astatine	86 Rn 222.0176* Radon
87 Fr 223.0197* Francium	88 Ra 226.0254* Radium	Ac-Lr 89 to 103 Actinides	104 Rf* 261.1087* Rutherfordium	105 Ha* 262.1138* Hahnium	106 Sg* 263.1182* Seaborgium	107 Ns* 262.1229* Nielsbohrium	108 Hs* Hassium	109 Mt* Meitnerium									

Lanthanide Series

57 La 138.9055 Lanthanum	58 Ce 140.115 Cerium	59 Pr 140.90765 Praseodymium	60 Nd 144.24 Neodymium	61 Pm 146.9151* Promethium	62 Sm 150.36 Samarium	63 Eu 151.965 Europium	64 Gd 157.25 Gadolinium	65 Tb 158.92534 Terbium	66 Dy 162.50 Dysprosium	67 Ho 164.93032 Holmium	68 Er 167.26 Erbium	69 Tm 168.93421 Thulium	70 Yb 173.04 Ytterbium	71 Lu 174.967 Lutetium

Actinide Series

89 Ac 227.0278* Actinium	90 Th 232.0381 Thorium	91 Pa 231.0359* Protactinium	92 U 238.0289 Uranium	93 Np 237.0482* Neptunium	94 Pu 244.0642* Plutonium	95 Am* 243.0614* Americium	96 Cm* 247.0703* Curium	97 Bk* 247.0703* Berkelium	98 Cf* 251.0796* Californium	99 Es* 252.0829* Einsteinium	100 Fm* 257.0951* Fermium	101 Md* 258.0986* Mendelevium	102 No* 259.1009* Nobelium	103 Lr* 260.1053* Lawrencium

ELEMENTAL NAMES

The elements and their atoms are identified by their atomic numbers 1 to 109 and by one- or two-letter symbols such as "O" for oxygen and "He" for helium. The numbers and symbols of the elements shown in the Periodic Table are used all over the world even though the names of the chemical elements are different in different languages.

Some elements were named for people (both real and mythical), and some were named for places. Curium (Cm) was named for Marie and Pierre Curie, who were pioneers in the field of radioactivity. Thorium (Th) was named for Thor, the Scandinavian god of war. Berkelium (Bk) is named after the city of Berkeley in California in the United States, and californium (Cf) is for the state itself. Francium (Fr) was named after the country of France, and europium (Eu) for the continent of Europe.

Some elements have even been named after planets. The planet Uranus was the source of the name for the element uranium (U). There are several other examples of elements named after planets. Look at the Periodic Table to see if you can find them. (HINT: Look at elements with higher atomic numbers.) On the other hand, one country was, in a way, named after an element. Argentina is a country in South America and was named from the Latin word *argentium*, which means silver. We use the symbol Ag for this metal.

You can use the symbols for the elements to play some word games. See if you can write your name using only chemical symbols. One of the authors of this book can spell his last name in two different chemical ways: BAtEs = boron, astatine, and einsteinium or BaTeS = barium, tellurium, and sulphur.

Can you find other words that can be written using only the chemical symbols? There are a few examples shown in the drawing on this page.

You can even write short sentences using only the elemental symbols. For example, did you know that GaSOLiNe CoNTaInS CaRbON?

PrOBaBiLiTiEs
ReSPONSiBiLiTiEs
NATuRaLISTiC
ScAtTeRbRaIn
PArIS
ClAsSiFICaTioN
UNiVErSiTiEs

ThErMoDyNAmICS
AmPLiFICaTiON
HAILuCINaTiON
OsTeNTaTiOUS
LiSBON
CoUNTeReSPIONaGe
ScHoLaSTiC

CHEMICAL MAPS

The wealth of the world can be displayed on a chemical map that shows the location and the quantity of each of the 94 natural elements. All food, clothing, and shelter for people, as well as their luxuries, are made of these elements. A chemical map of the United Kingdom is being prepared from satellite photographs and chemical analyses of the soil, rocks, and streams. The information is stored in computers and used for planning farms, mines, factories, roads, and parks. Similar chemical maps are planned for Canada and the United States.

You can make an element map of a room in your house. List the materials used in the floor, walls, ceiling, windows, doors, and of some of the objects in your room. For each material ask: "Is it animal, vegetable, or mineral?"

The main elements in "animal" materials are hydrogen, carbon, oxygen, nitrogen, sulphur, phosphorus, and calcium because these make up muscle and bone. The main "vegetable" elements are carbon, hydrogen, and oxygen that make up plants. The main "mineral" elements are the 73 metal elements in the Periodic Table. All of the elements (except hydrogen) that are located to the left of the heavy zigzag line in the Periodic Table are metals. The metals in your room may be found alone as iron or aluminum, as mixtures with other metals called alloys as in brass (copper and zinc), or as compounds with nonmetal elements as in table salt (sodium and chlorine). You might even have a synthetic element in your room—americium is in many smoke detectors.

After you have written down the elements you think are present in the materials and objects in your list, make a map of your room. On the map, write the names or symbols of the elements where they belong. You could colour each element a different colour. This will help you estimate how much of each element is present. You can also make a copy of the blank Periodic Table on page 78 of this book and mark in the elements you have identified in your room.

If you want to find out more information about the different elements (and compounds made from them), you can find reference books in the public library. One very useful reference book is the *Merck Index*, which contains information about 10,000 chemicals. You can also find information about the elements in the *CRC Handbook of Chemistry and Physics*.

Elements at Home

HOME
SWEET
HOME

Of the natural elements, only 17 are so unreactive that they do not readily combine with other elements. The rest are usually found combined with other elements in millions and millions of different chemical compounds.

A number of these elements can be located in and around your home. Carbon appears as diamonds used in jewellery, as needles for record players, as charcoal, and as graphite in pencils. Aluminum is used as foil for wrapping food, iron is used in pots and pans and nails, nickel is made into Canadian dimes and quarters, and copper is made into pennies, wire, and pipes. Zinc is found on the outside of some kinds of flashlight batteries. Zinc is also part of "flashing," which is sheets of material fitted around chimneys to keep rain from going through the roof. Gold and silver are used in jewellery, dentistry, and electronic equipment. Platinum is used in jewellery and is also found in the catalytic converter in automobile exhaust systems. Mercury is the liquid metal in thermometers, and lead is the soft, heavy metal hung on fishing lines to sink them in water. Elements that are gases are also found in your home. Most of the air is nitrogen, but you need the oxygen in the air to live. If you have a balloon in your room that is floating in the air, you even have some helium in your home.

OXYGEN

Over 200 years ago, a French chemist named Antoine Lavoisier was the first to measure the percentage of oxygen in air. You can repeat his experiment using simple materials from the kitchen.

Use a knife and a fork to pack a pad of steel wool into the bottom of a clear jar or glass. Avoid touching the sharp steel wool with your bare fingers. Rinse the steel wool thoroughly with tap water and then invert the jar in a pan or bowl half full of water. If the jar will not stand up or starts to float, remove some of the water. Put a rubber band around the jar. You will use it later to mark the water level.

The steel wool will become rusty as it reacts with the oxygen in the air in the jar. Rust is a solid compound of iron and oxygen (iron oxide). As the oxygen is removed from the air in the jar to form rust, the volume of the air remaining in the jar gets smaller and smaller, and the water rises inside the jar to replace the oxygen. After standing for about four hours, the water level in the jar will rise above the water level in the bowl. In about 12 hours, the water level will stop rising

because all the oxygen has been used to make rust.

Leave the jar in the bowl and add water to the bowl till it reaches the same level as the water in the jar. This makes the pressure on the air remaining in the jar the same as the pressure of the air outside. Now you can compare the volume of air you have left with the volume of air you started with. Mark this final water level with the rubber band and then turn the jar right side up, leaving the rusty steel wool in the jar. Measure the volume of the oxygen-free air you had left in the jar by filling the jar up to the rubber band with water from a measuring cup.

Now measure the volume of the air you started with, before the oxygen reacted, by filling the bottle right to the top with water. The difference between the two volumes of water is the amount of oxygen that was in the air before it reacted with the steel wool. Lavoisier found air to be about one fifth or 20% oxygen by volume. Compare your measurement with his.

Sometimes people's lungs cannot extract as much oxygen as they need from the air they breathe. When this happens, they must breathe air that has extra oxygen added to it, or sometimes even pure oxygen. They can get this extra oxygen from special oxygen tanks.

GOLD

Gold is perhaps the best known of all the 94 natural chemical elements. A piece of gold shines and feels warm and heavy in your hand. For most of history, people have considered gold to be very valuable. In many countries, gold is the standard for measuring how much money is worth—a certain amount of money will buy a certain amount of gold. The chemical symbol for gold is Au, from its Latin name *aurum*, which means "shining dawn."

Since ancient times, people have used a piece of rock called a touchstone to help them recognize gold and other minerals and metals. You can do this test yourself with a white quartz pebble. Any shiny white stone you find is probably quartz, or you can find quartz stones in aquarium gravel.

Scratch the pebble with a penny and a quarter. The penny leaves a shiny red streak of copper and the quarter leaves a silvery streak of nickel. Try this test with pieces of coloured foil to see what streaks they leave. Gold will leave a buttery yellow streak, but gold is very soft and will scratch easily, so don't use gold for this test. Geologists test minerals in this way with streak plates made of baked white clay. Almost every mineral gives its own kind of streak and that helps the scientists identify them.

Gold is called a noble metal, not because it is used for royal jewellery, but because it does not readily combine with other substances. It acts the same way as noble people of the past, who did not mix with ordinary people. Almost all the gold that has ever been found on earth has been efficiently recycled because it is so valuable. The total amount of gold collected by people to date is estimated at 100,000 tonnes (tons). This would fill a cube that is 17 metres (55 feet) on each edge, or about the size of a five-storey building.

As well as being soft and easily scratched, gold is also malleable. It can be bent into different shapes, such as rings, and it can be pounded into very thin sheets called gold leaf. A one-centimetre (0.4 inch) cube of gold can be pounded into a thin sheet that would cover 20 square metres (215 square feet). Gold leaf has been used for centuries in art, to decorate books, to cover statues, and even to cover parts of buildings. Gold will not tarnish, so it makes a good decorative cover.

To make gold harder, it is alloyed with other metals such as silver, copper, and zinc. The amount of gold in alloys is measured in carats; 24 carat gold is pure gold, and 18 carat gold is 18/24ths pure or 75% gold.

Gold does not damage living cells, so it is used for filling and repairing teeth. A thin layer of gold is very reflective, so it is used on the visors of space helmets to protect astronauts from harmful solar radiation. It is also used in electronics because it is a good conductor of electricity and does not corrode.

SILVER

Like its cousin gold, silver has been used and treasured for centuries. There are silver mines in the world that have been in use for hundreds of years and are still producing silver. Silver is a beautiful, shiny metal used for jewellery and expensive tableware.

The Latin word for silver is *argentium.* It is also the origin of the chemical symbol for silver, Ag. The name of Argentina, a country in South America, comes from silver's Latin name.

Cutlery and dishes made from silver are called silverware. Silverware tarnishes even when it is not used every day because it slowly reacts with traces of hydrogen sulfide that are in the air. Silver can be polished to restore its shiny surface. You can carry out the chemical reaction that causes tarnishing without damaging silverware.

Hard boil an egg and put the yellow ball of egg yolk on a polished silver spoon. After about two days, you will see a ring of tarnish on the silver all around the egg yolk. This brown-black chemical compound is silver sulfide, Ag_2S. It is formed from silver and hydrogen sulfide gas, H_2S. In this case, the H_2S comes from the boiled egg yolk. The dark ring is easily removed from the spoon by rubbing it with a cloth.

Sterling silver is 92.5% silver and 7.5% copper or another metal that is mixed or alloyed with the silver to make it wear longer. More than half of the 15 million kilograms (16,500 tons) of silver mined in the world each year is used to make photographic film. The second largest use is for electronic equipment such as computers and stereo equipment because silver conducts heat and electricity better than any other metal. Silver is also used in musical instruments like flutes because it produces such a lovely tone.

COPPER

Pure copper is easily stretched, bent, and hammered very thin. To make it harder, other metals are mixed with the copper to make alloys. About 6,000 years ago, people made one of the greatest scientific discoveries when they learned how to make bronze by mixing tin with copper. Both tin and copper were too soft to be used for tools or weapons. But bronze was much harder and could make a sharp edge. So people no longer had to use clumsy stone tools for hunting, cutting trees, and harvesting crops.

Pennies and water pipes are made from copper alloys, but electrical wires are made from pure copper. This is because any impurities in the copper would increase the resistance of the wires to the flow of electricity. This resistance would cause the electricity to be wasted as heat, and it would also create a fire hazard. Most of the copper that is mined is used in power lines and electrical equipment.

When exposed to air, copper darkens or tarnishes and becomes covered with a very thin film of brown compounds of copper and oxygen. You can see this film on old pennies, and you can remove it by treating the coins with vinegar.

Find two dark old pennies and a shiny new one and soak one of the old pennies in vinegar for about 20 minutes. Now wash the soaked penny thoroughly in water and rub it dry with a soft cloth. Compare the three coins, and you

Oops, not enough tin in that sword!

will see that you have brightened up the old one.

Very old copper surfaces exposed to moist air, such as the roofs and outdoor drain pipes on old buildings, react with water and the carbon dioxide and sulphur dioxide in the air to form a green coating. You can see this coating on the roofs of old buildings like the Hotel Vancouver, in Vancouver, Canada, and on statues like the Statue of Liberty in New York City in the United States. You can sometimes see the green coating in sinks and bathrooms where copper pipes have dripped water. This stain can also be cleaned with vinegar, as your pennies were. Put vinegar or a cloth soaked in vinegar on the stain. Gently rubbing the stain will speed up the cleaning reaction. You can clean stains from copper-bottomed cooking pots this way too.

ALUMINUM

Aluminum is the most plentiful metal on earth. It is found as a compound with oxygen (making it an oxide) that makes up one kind of clay. To isolate the aluminum, chemicals called fluorides are mixed with the clay and an electrical current is sent through the mixture. The energy from the current causes a chemical reaction that releases the aluminum. This happens at such a high temperature that the aluminum melts and can be drained off into moulds to cool.

When aluminum was first separated in the mid-1800s, it was so valuable that plates and cutlery were made from it for some very rich people. Napoleon III, emperor of France, was very proud of his aluminum tableware. Aluminum is no longer regarded as a luxury because the modern method of separating aluminum has made it very plentiful.

Aluminum is light and very strong, so it is used to make cans, boats, airplanes, and bicycles. It is also used to make cookie sheets, cooking pots, and other baking equipment. You can probably find many things made of aluminum in your home.

Aluminum is also used to make foil, often used to wrap leftover food. Because one side of aluminum foil is shiny, it can be used to make a solar collector. Line a mixing bowl with aluminum foil with the shiny side up and press the foil as smooth as possible. Bend the ends of the sheet over the edge of the bowl to hold the lining in place. Dig a shallow hole in some loose soil in your garden and place the bowl in it so it is facing the sun. In a few minutes, put your hand in the bowl. You will find that the air in the bowl will feel warmer than the air outside.

When sunlight enters your solar collector, it is reflected to a spot just above the centre of the bowl, called the focus. Because there are so many solar rays concentrated in one spot, the air gets very hot. Nomads in Asia use a similar solar collector that they carry with them to make tea without having to light a fire. They use a solar collector mirror about 2 metres (6 feet) wide. When a kettle of water is hung in the focus of the collector, the water will eventually boil.

Other bowl-shaped collectors can also be found in nature. Some arctic flowers have pale-colored, bowl-shaped blossoms that turn to follow the sun. Bees pollinate the flowers by flying from one to another and they cuddle down inside the blossoms to keep warm.

CARBON

What is colourless and hard, black and powdery, grey and slippery, and the world's tiniest soccer balls? Carbon, depending on the arrangement of its atoms, can exist as diamonds, soot, graphite, or as tiny balls of sixty carbon atoms, which look much like a soccer ball. Carbon is perhaps the most important of all the elements because it is the building material for all living things.

About 85% of the earth's 45 million tonnes (tons) of carbon is found in the oceans, 9% in the ground, and about 4% in plants and animals. Just 2% of the earth's carbon is present in the air as carbon dioxide gas. Carbon dioxide is exhaled by people and animals, and is "breathed in" by plants. It is also released into the air when something burns or decays.

Chemists have invented or discovered more than fifteen million different kinds of carbon-containing molecules. Carbon is a very special element because its atoms can so easily join to other carbon atoms. In plants and animals the carbon atoms are commonly joined together in chain-like molecules. Besides forming chains of atoms, carbon

atoms can also link to each other to make a cyclic molecule, and the rings can join to each other to make a flat pattern much like the tiles on a bathroom floor. You have probably seen two forms of carbon called allotropes: graphite and diamonds. Graphite is many layers of these flat carbon rings. The carbon atoms in each layer are strongly bonded to each other, but the layers easily slide over each other. Graphite is used to lubricate things like squeaky hinges or locks that don't turn smoothly. It is also mixed with clay to make pencil lead. When we write with a pencil, layers of carbon atom rings slide off the pencil lead onto the paper to leave a dark mark.

Press a piece of putty on top of a pencilled word. The putty will remove some of the graphite, and

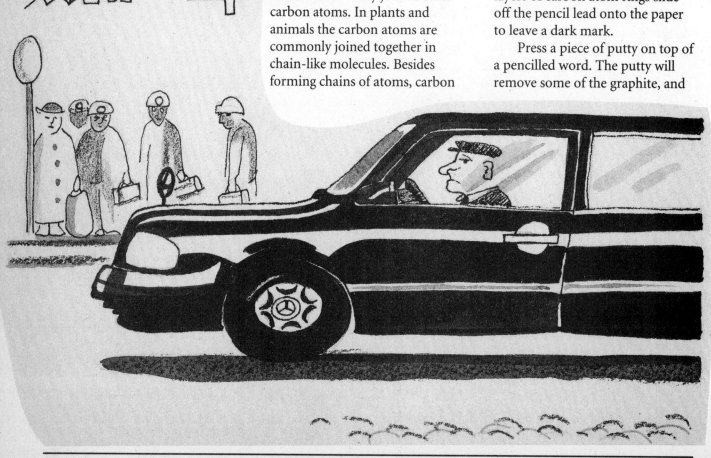

you will see the word written backwards on the putty. You can remove another layer from the same pencil mark by pressing it with fresh putty, and you may even be able to remove a third or a fourth layer.

Surprisingly to many people, the same chemical element that is soft black soot or slippery gray graphite is also what makes a diamond. Diamonds are also pure carbon and are the hardest substance in the world. The name diamond comes from a Greek word meaning "untameable." A diamond is hard because of its molecular structure. In a diamond, each ring of six carbon atoms is puckered into a shape that looks a little bit like a chair. The chair-rings are bonded to each other just as strongly as the atoms in the rings. Because all the carbon atoms in a diamond crystal are tightly bonded together into one giant three-dimensional molecule, a diamond is the largest and strongest single molecule in the world.

In the form of a diamond, carbon has long been used in jewellery. The Cullinan diamond, found in South Africa in 1905, was the largest diamond ever mined. It weighed 3,106 carats or 621 grams (22 ounces) before it was cut into gems. The largest diamond gem, one of the British Crown Jewels, weighs 106 grams (3.8 ounces). Microdiamonds, less than a millimetre (0.04 inches) long, have been found in Alberta, Saskatchewan, the Northwest Territories, and in meteorites. The first synthetic diamonds were made in 1962 by heating graphite to 5,000°C (9,000°F) under a pressure 200,000 times the pressure of the atmosphere. Synthetic diamonds are not large enough for jewellery, but are used in knives, saws, and drills for cutting through hard substances such as rock, steel, glass, and teeth.

MAGNET METALS

A magnet is a device that strongly attracts chemical elements called ferromagnetic metals—iron, nickel, and cobalt. Magnets are often made from iron, but can also be made from alloys. Magnets have two areas that attract ferromagnetic elements. These areas are called the north and south poles.

The north pole of a magnet will attract the south pole of another magnet (because unlike poles attract). But two like poles (S and S or N and N) will repel each other. An object made from a ferromagnetic metal will be attracted to either end of a magnet.

A compass needle is a permanent magnet that is balanced so it can turn easily in any direction. The Chinese invented the compass about 1,700 years ago and used it to steer ships on the sea when they were out of sight of land. North of the equator, the north end of a compass needle will always point to the North Magnetic Pole of the earth, which is in arctic Canada. South of the equator, the south end of a compass needle will point to the South Magnetic Pole.

To make your own compass, magnetize a sewing needle by stroking it several times from the eye of the needle to its point with a bar magnet, one end of a horseshoe magnet, or even a refrigerator magnet. Push the needle-magnet through a cork or a small ball of white polystyrene about the size of the top of your thumb till both ends of the needle can be seen. Float the ball or cork in a glass or plastic bowl filled with water. It will come to rest with the north pole of the needle pointing to the earth's North Magnetic Pole.

Many metal objects found in your home are ferromagnetic. To test these objects, bring them close to your compass and see if they attract, repel, or have no effect on the needle. You can also try to magnetize knives and other metal objects. Check different denominations of coins to see which ones are ferromagnetic. You can compare the strength of your magnets by seeing how many ferromagnetic coins they can pick up.

'Bout time they cleaned up some of their garbage!

3 Water, A Simple Compound

Scientists have discovered that none of the atoms that make up the elements are destroyed when substances are transformed in chemical reactions. On earth, atoms are constantly recycled from one kind of material into another. All living things grow, die, decay, and grow again from the same atoms through chemical changes.

Generally, all atoms, except those of the six Noble Gases found in the extreme right-hand column of the Periodic Table, combine with each other to form compounds that make up all of the many different things in our world. The atoms in all of these compounds are held together by chemical bonds made up of even smaller particles called electrons. In chemical reactions, the electrons change places and make new bonds with different atoms to produce new compounds.

Each compound has a different combination of atoms that is shown by a formula such as H_2O for water (2 hydrogen atoms and 1 oxygen atom) and CO_2 for carbon dioxide (1 carbon atom and 2 oxygen atoms). Chemists record about 3,000 new compounds every week. In your body alone you have over five million different compounds!

In this chapter you will find out about one of the simplest and most abundant compounds, water, and about some of the changes which it can undergo. Most scientists agree that life started in the sea, and some plants and animals later came ashore and learned to live on land. When they came ashore, they brought water with them in each of their living cells. About two-thirds of your body is water.

Life on earth depends on water. Plants use solar energy to combine water and carbon dioxide in their leaves to form sugars. The sugars dissolve in the water that was collected by the roots to make sap. These sugars are carried in the sap to the growing cells of the plant, where they are converted into fruit, stems, leaves, and roots. Animals and people eat the plants, and their blood carries the sugars to their cells. There the stored solar energy in the sugars is released when they are converted back into carbon dioxide and water.

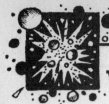

WATER QUESTIONS

The following experiments will show you some surprising properties of water and help you understand the importance of water.

1. Can water climb uphill?

Very fine tubes are called capillaries. The blue veins you can see in your wrists are examples of capillaries. Another capillary is the plastic ink tube in a ballpoint pen. Take out the tube from an old pen and cut off the writing end. Touch the end of this capillary tube to the surface of water dyed with a few drops of food colouring. The water will climb up into the tube all by itself. Now lift the tube out of the water. The water will not run out even though both ends of the tube are open. Stand a rolled-up paper towel in half a glass of water and the water will climb uphill in the fine capillaries in the paper right to the top of the towel.

To understand why water climbs up the walls of capillaries, you need to know about the shape of water molecules. Even though they cannot see water molecules, chemists have determined their shape through many different experiments.

A water molecule (H_2O) is V-shaped, with the oxygen (O) atom at the bottom of the V and the two hydrogen (H) atoms at the ends of the arms. The electrons that glue the atoms together in the molecule stay close to the oxygen atom. This gives the oxygen atom a partial negative charge. As a result,

the hydrogen end of the molecule is somewhat positively charged.

Chemists believe that the positive and negative ends of neighbouring water molecules attract each other and form a three

dimensional network. In other words, the water "sticks" to itself. It is this property of water that makes it rise in a fine tube and stay there.

Because the molecules of plants and anything made from plants also have negative oxygen atoms bonded to positive hydrogen atoms, water can stick to these materials as well. The attraction between molecules of wood and molecules of water is so strong that water is pulled uphill against gravity even to the tops of the tallest trees.

2. Can you carry a glass of water upside down?

Do this experiment over a sink or outside. Cover a glass of water with a water-proof card. You could cut the card from a milk carton or a stiff sheet of plastic. Hold the card in place over the top of the glass while you turn it upside down. Now remove your hand from the card. The water will not run out. Repeat the experiment but change the amount of water in the glass from full to a very small amount. Make small nailholes in the card and try it again. The water will still not run out.

Many people guess that the pressure of the air on the waterproof card seals the water in the glass, but if you look closely, you will see that the card is not tight up against the rim of the glass. It actually hangs below it on a thin film of water. Since air can easily pass in and out of the glass through the nailholes or the water film, it is easy to see that air pressure is not the only reason why water will not run out of the upside-down glass. It is the self-stickiness of water that keeps it in the upside-down glass and prevents it from running out small holes.

3. How does water behave with static electricity?

Rub a plastic comb on some wool to give the comb a negative electric charge. Bring the comb close to a thin stream of water from a tap. The stream will bend towards the negative electrical charge on the plastic.

Now rub a piece of glass with silk. This will give the glass a positive electric charge. Bring the piece of glass close to the stream of water and observe what happens. The stream of water will also bend towards the positive electric charge. Because water has both a negative and positive electrical charge, it is attracted to both the negative charge of the comb and the positive charge of the glass.

4. What happens to water and ice in a microwave oven?

Put a few cubes of ice in one cup and about the same volume of water in another cup. Place the

two cups together in a microwave oven on high for about 90 seconds. After 90 seconds, the water will be boiling but the ice cubes will not even have started to melt.

Molecules of water in ice are held together more tightly in their three-dimensional network than when they are in liquid form. When molecules of liquid water absorb microwaves in a microwave oven, they rotate. The rotation of the molecules heats the water until it boils, and some of the molecules escape from the liquid as steam. Microwaves cook food by heating the water inside it. But microwaves cannot easily rotate the water molecules in ice because they are held too tightly in their solid network.

SNOW

If snow and water are both made of molecules of water, why can we see through water but not through snow?

Snowflakes are ice crystals formed from water vapour in the clouds. It is said that no two snowflakes are exactly alike.

When snow is piled on the ground, light shining through it does not follow a straight path. The light is bent by each ice crystal (snowflake). Since there are many crystals lying in a helter-skelter heap, the light is bent in many different directions. The light that gets through the snow appears as a glow because it is entering your eyes from many different directions. You cannot see an object through the snow because the light from the object is broken and bent before it gets to your eyes. The next time you play in the snow, dig a little cave in the side of a snowbank and look at the glow of light that comes through the snow.

Snow has other interesting properties. When snowflakes fall to the ground, they pile up in white jumbles of snowflakes and air is trapped between them. Snow is about 90% air. This trapped air cannot move and carry heat away, so a snow cave will warm up from the heat of a body. This property has saved the lives of people who have been lost in blizzards. They dug caves and stayed in them to keep from freezing. This is the same principle that keeps people warm inside an igloo.

The trapped air in snow also muffles noise. Sound needs air movement, and since the air in snow cannot readily move, it doesn't carry noise to your ears.

To measure the amount of air in snow, put a glass outside when it is snowing. When it is full, bring it inside and let the snow melt. Snow is about 90% air, so 10 centimetres (or 10 inches) of snow should make about one centimetre (or 1 inch) of melted water.

ICE

Ice floats in water because the water molecules are held further apart in ice than in liquid water, making ice less dense than water. If ice did not float, oceans and lakes would freeze from the bottom up and all aquatic life on earth would be killed.

You can lift a floating ice cube out of a glass of water with a piece of string. Wet the end of the string and lay the wet part on the ice cube. Now sprinkle the ice cube with a pinch of salt. In about 15 seconds, the string will freeze to the ice, and you can pull the cube out of the glass with the string.

In winter, salt is sprinkled on sidewalks to melt snow and ice, so how is it that salt freezes the string to the ice in your experiment? The answer to this question comes from the V-shape of water molecules and their negative and positive charges.

Salt crystals are three-dimensional networks of sodium atoms that have a positive electric charge and chlorine atoms that have a negative electric charge. Atoms with electric charges are called ions. Since opposite electric charges attract each other, when salt is sprinkled on ice, the ions of the salt attract the water molecules of the ice crystals with their negative and positive ends. A little bit of the ice melts, and the salt dissolves in the melt water.

On a snow-covered sidewalk, the heat needed for melting the snow or ice is supplied from the air and the sidewalk. In your

experiment, the sprinkled salt melts the parts of the ice cube on either side of the string, and the heat needed for melting is taken out of the wet string causing it to freeze against the unmelted part of the ice cube.

If you put the salt on the ice cube *before* you lay on the wet string, they will not freeze together. This is because the salt melts the ice under the string and makes it into salt water, which freezes only at a temperature below 0°C (32°F), the temperature at which water freezes. That is also why the salty oceans do not freeze in winter.

ICE AND SOLAR ENERGY

We use ice to keep ourselves and our food and drinks cool. This is because ice absorbs heat energy. Heat from the sun is solar energy. It keeps the earth warm and suitable for life.

Here is an easy way for you to measure the heat that comes to the earth from the sun. An instrument for measuring heat is called a calorimeter, and you can use a bag of ice as a solar calorimeter. Put about 5 millilitres (1 teaspoon) of water in one corner of a transparent plastic sandwich bag and tie a knot in the bag to seal it. Make a hole through the bag above the knot, and slip a straw through the hole. Hang the bag in a transparent glass wide-mouthed jar by resting the straw across the top. Make sure the bag does not touch the jar. Put the jar and bag in the freezer compartment of your refrigerator.

When the water in the bag has frozen into a solid lump of ice, put the jar outdoors in the sun, making a note of the time. Examine your calorimeter frequently and note the exact time when the ice has completely melted.

The solar energy taken up by the ice removes water molecules from their positions in the ice crystals. This lets them move about freely as liquid water. Ice does not heat up while it is melting. Instead, the ice and water mixture remains at exactly 0°C (32°F), freezing temperature, until all of the ice has melted. The shorter the time it takes to melt the piece of ice, the larger the amount of solar heat that has reached that place on earth during that time. You can measure the effects of clouds on solar energy by refreezing the same sample of water and comparing the times it takes to melt on sunny and cloudy days.

The amount of energy coming to you from the sun changes with the time of day, the time of year, and your location on the earth. In the northern hemisphere at noon on about June 21, the sun is at its highest above your head. So the sunlight has the shortest path to come through the atmosphere and more solar energy reaches you than at any other time of the year.

SALT WATER AND THE SUN

Heat from the sun can purify water. The apparatus for doing this is called a solar still. Plastic solar stills are kept in lifeboats so shipwrecked people can make fresh drinking water from salty seawater.

To see how a solar still works, dissolve some table salt in water and add a drop of green food colouring to make imitation seawater. Put about 15 millilitres (1 tablespoon) of the green solution in a shallow plastic dish and place the dish inside a clear plastic bag. Gently inflate the bag by blowing air into it through a drinking straw, then slip out the straw and seal the bag with a twist-tie. Put the bag and dish in the sunlight and protect them from the wind.

The sun evaporates water from the dish. This water vapour rises, then condenses into water again when it hits the top of the bag. Then the liquid water runs down into the bottom corner of the bag. After a few hours, you can remove the distilled water by cutting off the lower corner of the bag with scissors, and you can drink the clean, fresh water.

You can also get drinking water on a sunny day, even in a desert. Dig a hole in the ground, put a cup in the bottom of the hole, and cover the hole with a transparent sheet of plastic. The sun evaporates water from the sides of the hole and the water vapour condenses on the underside of the plastic. If you put a stone in the centre of the plastic sheet, it will guide the drops of pure water into the cup.

SALT AND WATER

Salt comes from the sea. In hot climates it is harvested by letting seawater evaporate in shallow ponds. Salt mines are found where dried up seas have been covered with soil and rock. In the mines, salt crystals can grow to be very large.

In the previous experiment, you distilled drinking water from salty water. In this experiment, you'll find that it is also possible to separate salt from water. With care and patience, you can grow your own large crystals of pure salt (sodium chloride, NaCl) that shine and glitter like diamonds.

Salt crystals grow best in a saturated brine, that is, water that has dissolved as much salt as it can hold. Brine in an open dish remains saturated because the water evaporates as the crystals grow.

Stir one part of table salt with three parts of water for about five minutes. Then filter the brine through a layer of paper tissue into a transparent dish. Set the open container on black paper in a sunny window. Drop in a grain of salt to act as a seed for the crystal growth. In a few hours, gleaming, transparent crystals of salt will appear in the container. These will continue to grow for many days as the water slowly evaporates into the air.

Table salt is not pure sodium chloride, but has small amounts of extra ingredients added to make the salt flow freely and to improve your health. See the label on the box. These extra ingredients make the brine cloudy and interfere with the way the dissolved salt particles fit themselves onto the growing crystal surfaces. Therefore, it is best to remove as many of these impurities as possible.

To purify the sodium chloride, pour off and discard the brine (the mother liquor). Then redissolve the crystals in a little tap water, add a seed crystal, and regrow the crystals. The second mother liquor will not be as cloudy as the first. By repeating this process, you will eventually obtain beautiful, big, sparkling crystals.

4 Bubbles & Soap

Soap is an interesting compound that has a much larger and more complex molecule than water does. Each soap molecule is usually a chain of 16 or 18 carbon atoms coated on the outside with hydrogen atoms. At one end of the molecule, called the "head," the end carbon atom is joined to two oxygen atoms. These oxygen atoms are attracted to water. The rest of the soap molecule, made of only carbon and hydrogen atoms, is called the "tail." It is chemically similar to oil, and like oil, does not mix with water. But because it is like oil, it is attracted to oils and fats, which are chemically almost identical to each other. Therefore soap molecules partly dissolve in water (the heads) and partly dissolve in oil (the tails) at the same time to form a kind of bridge between these two different substances.

Greasy dishes can be cleaned with soap and water. The soap's tails dissolve in the grease (oil), while the soap's heads stay dissolved in the water. The soap helps to remove oily material from the dishes. Dirty hands and clothes are soiled with "dirt" mixed with a little oil that often comes from your skin. This dirt is cleaned away with the help of the soap's double ability of being attracted to both water and oil at the same time. The combination of soap and oil can be washed away with water, and this is how soap cleans our clothes, dishes, and bodies.

TOSSING BUBBLES

Soap bubbles are beautiful and fun to play with. You can make the best bubbles in cool, shady, moist places sheltered from the wind. If you make bubbles near buildings or trees, they might ride updrafts called "thermals" into the sky.

The biggest and best bubbles are made, not by blowing, but by tossing them from a bubble loop. Make your bubble mixture in a tray. Mix together 1,250 millilitres (5 cups) of water, 125 mL (1/2 cup) of liquid detergent, 25 mL (2 tablespoons) of vegetable cooking oil, and 7.5 mL (1/2 tablespoon) of rubbing alcohol (isopropyl alcohol). Remember not to taste anything and to wash your hands after you make the mixture.

You can make a bubble loop from pipe cleaners bent into a flat ring with a handle like a frying pan. You can also make larger loops from wire coat hangers that you wrap strips of cheesecloth around as a cover. You may also buy a bubble loop in a toystore.

Dip the loop into the bubble mixture and then slide it out gently to form a soap film across the ring. Raise the ring forward and upward in a smooth motion like flipping a pancake. A large bubble will form under the ring in still air and, as you complete the toss, it will roll off the front of the ring and drift upwards and away.

The walls of bubbles are made from two soap films, an inner one and an outer one, with a layer of water in between them. When the

water drains to the bottom of the bubble—POOF!—the bubble bursts. The alcohol and the vegetable oil in the middle water layer between the two soap film layers of the bubble slow down the drainage of water to make the bubble last longer.

Try to catch your bubble on the loop and re-toss it. Or play bubble volleyball with a friend by trying to keep the bubble floating by blowing on it.

If you can draw out a long bubble between two bubble loops, it takes the shape of a cylinder with round ends, somewhat like a sausage. When the length of the cylinder becomes more than twice the distance around it, the long bubble divides in the middle all by itself into two bubbles. Scientists who study living cells have used this automatic behaviour of long bubbles as a model to explain how rod-shaped, one-celled bacteria can divide themselves into two daughter bacteria without tearing open their cell walls.

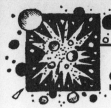

SOAP AND CELLS

You can make a soap film on water that is so thin, it is invisible. You will be able to see where the film is because it pushes small floating particles away and leaves the water surface looking clean.

Fill a large mixing bowl with water and lightly dust talcum powder or powdered chalk on the surface of the water. Dip a toothpick into liquid soap or detergent and wipe off any excess. Then touch the toothpick to the centre of the powder layer. In a flash, the powder will be pushed away to leave a clear circle. Measure the diameter of the circle.

Many other things in your house are also soaps—toothpaste, shampoo, and hand soap. Make films with these different products and compare how far they spread the powder in a circle on the surface of water.

If soap molecules are not disturbed, they will spread out on the surface of water until they form a film one molecule deep. The oil tails of the molecules stand up together on top of the water, like grass on a lawn. The heads of the molecules stay in the water. Soap films that are one molecule deep are called "monolayer" films.

Sometimes, two soap films will join together to make a "bilayer." In a bilayer, the two sheets of molecule tails are close together in the middle and the heads are on the two outer surfaces.

Bilayer soap films are similar to the outer walls of all living cells. The cell wall acts as a filter to let some chemicals in and other chemicals out. Molecules of certain chemicals are attached to cell walls in your body and act like identifying markers that tell other cells that these cells are "you" (that is, they belong to your body). Cells such as bacteria and germs that come from outside your body will have the wrong markers. These are recognized as foreign cells and removed from your body before they can harm you. This is one way your body keeps you healthy.

I'm tellin' ya, I was just in the wrong place at the wrong time....

BUBBLE SANDWICHES

Mathematicians describe a sugar cube as a square prism. This means that it has a square top and bottom and four square sides, the same as a baby's toy block. A glass prism used for making rainbows is a triangular prism. A triangular prism looks like a tent that has three rectangles—two sides and the bottom—and a triangle at each end. There are more complex prisms with five, six, seven, or even more sides.

When a foam of bubbles is trapped between two plastic sheets, like the sides of a plastic sandwich bag, the bubbles are attracted to the plastic and tend to stick to it. The bubbles change from spheres and become prisms with their tops and bottoms attached to the plastic. These prisms will have three to eight or more flat sides.

You can do this experiment in a transparent plastic bag and watch the bubbles change. Put approximately 25 millilitres (2 tablespoons) of a bubble mixture (see "Tossing Bubbles") in the corner of a clear plastic sandwich bag. Dip a drinking straw into the liquid and blow bubbles to half fill the bag. Remove the straw and seal the bag. You will be able to see the prism bubbles best if you add some food colouring to the bubble mixture before blowing the bubbles, and hang the bag in front of a window. When you hang the bag up, any water will run to the bottom. But the bubbles will stay attached to the sides of the plastic.

In the bubble sandwich, the

prisms grow and change shape as time passes. At first there may be a mixture of three, four, five, six or more sided bubble prisms. But as the foam ages over a day or so, all the bubbles will become six-sided with six-sided tops and bottoms. They are called hexagonal prisms. The prisms grow into hexagonal prisms according to a formula

discovered by the mathematician John von Neumann.

The cells of wax that bees make to form their honeycombs are similar in shape to the bubbles in your bubble sandwich. Nature seems to like the hexagon because it is a very efficient way to use space, and a number of hexagons fitted together is very strong.

KALEIDOSCOPE

A kaleidoscope is made of bits of coloured glass and mirrors inside a cardboard tube. When you look through the tube while turning it, you see changing patterns of colour. Here is how to make an automatic chemical kaleidoscope from a glass of milk, drops of liquid detergent, and food colouring.

Before you begin the experiment, lay down a piece of paper towel to put the toothpicks and food colouring on. Put some milk in a glass. The glass doesn't need to be deep, but choose one that is as wide as possible. Whole milk works best, but 1% and 2% will also do. You can use two or more different food colourings.

Dip one end of a toothpick in a food colouring and put a drop of the colouring in the centre of the milk. Dip the end of another toothpick in the liquid detergent and gently touch the food colouring. The food colouring will spread out into a ring near the wall of the glass. Repeat this using other food colourings. Finish off with the detergent.

Using another toothpick, put larger drops of detergent at three different places on the wall of the glass above the level of the milk. As the detergent seeps down onto the

milk, it will push the rings into swirls of colour on the milk surface. The pattern of colours will continue to change all by itself like an automatic kaleidoscope for about an hour. While this is happening, do not disturb the milk.

Milk is mostly water with tiny globules of butterfat (oil) suspended in it. Detergents are chemically similar to soap and are attracted to both water and oil. When the detergent molecules meet a fat globule in the milk, the tails of the soap molecules stick into the fat globule, but the heads stick out like the fluffy seeds of a ripe dandelion. These "dandelion balls" of fat and detergent are called *micelles*, and they keep the fat suspended in the water.

The drops of detergent you put on the surface of the milk spread out into a thin soap film that pushes away the molecules of food colouring (like the dust in "Soap and Cells"). Then the butterfat globules in the milk slowly form micelles with the detergent and help to remove it from the surface of the milk. So the food colouring spreads out again. As more detergent seeps down the wall of the glass, it pushes the food colouring into new patterns, and again the rising butterfat globules remove the detergent and the cycle starts all over again.

5 Chemical Changes

All of chemistry involves changes. Sometimes there are changes in the way in which the atoms that make up compounds are held together. These are called chemical reactions. Sometimes there are changes in the state of a material. These are physical changes like melting or freezing. Sometimes there are changes in the purity of a material. These are changes that may involve both chemical and physical changes.

Sometimes there are changes that you can see in a reaction, which make it easy to tell that a change is happening. For example, sometimes there may be a change in the colour of a material, or in its temperature, or perhaps bubbles may appear during a reaction. Sometimes it is hard to tell that a change is happening, and it is necessary to separate and analyze the reaction to see what, if anything, has occurred.

ACIDS AND BASES

In pure water, about one in every 500 million water molecules (H_2O) separates into a positively charged ion called a proton and a negatively charged ion called a hydroxide ion. (Ions are particles of matter that have an electrical charge.)

In pure water, the number of protons is exactly equal to the number of hydroxide ions. This means that the charges cancel each other out and the water is neutral. But if a substance is added to water that increases the number of protons, the water becomes acidic. If a substance adds more hydroxide ions, the water becomes basic.

Vinegar and lemon juice are acids because they can supply extra protons to water. Washing soda, ammonia, baking soda, and borax are bases because they produce extra hydroxide ions when they are added to water. We can mix these substances with water to make it acidic or basic and back again. You can see these changes in water by adding tiny amounts of a chemical called an "acid-base indicator." An acid-base indicator changes its colour when the solutions it is in are changed from acidic to basic or back again.

Some indicators are found in nature and others are made by chemists. Phenolphthalein is an acid-base indicator made by chemists. It is found in unflavoured Ex-lax tablets sealed in plastic cards.

To make your own acid-base indicator, crush one Ex-lax tablet inside its plastic wrapper. Then cut a slit in the wrapper and shake out some of the powder into a glass. Add 15 millilitres (1 tablespoon) of rubbing alcohol (isopropyl alcohol) and stir. Filter the yellow liquid through paper tissue into a bottle and label it "Phenolphthalein Indicator Solution." Remember to work safely and do not taste any of these substances and wash your hands thoroughly after mixing any solutions.

Make basic water solutions by separately dissolving a pinch each of baking soda and borax in 15 mL (1 tablespoon) of water. Add one drop of the indicator solution to each basic solution and swirl. The borax solution will turn bright pink. Baking soda is a weaker base than borax and will turn a paler pink colour.

When you stir two or three drops of white vinegar or lemon juice into the pink solution, it will become colourless. You can then stir in more base to bring back the pink colour, add more acid to remove it, and so on.

Magnesium hydroxide is a base that is sold as a white mixture with water called Milk of Magnesia. We have hydrochloric acid (HCl) in our stomachs. This acid helps digest our food, and sometimes after eating we may feel an unpleasant sensation called "heartburn," caused by too much acid. A simple treatment for this condition, recommended by doctors, is to neutralize some of the hydrochloric acid with a spoonful of Milk of Magnesia.

sure hope it works...

MILK OF MAGN

BLUE AND RED PLANT PIGMENTS

In this experiment, you will use an acid-base indicator found in nature. Anthocyanin is a pigment found in roses, violets, raspberries, purple cabbage, and many other plants. It is also an indicator because it changes colour when treated with acids and bases. You can do the following experiment with petals from roses or violets, but purple cabbage is often easier to get.

Shred a little purple cabbage and stir it in half a glass of water. Filter the purple solution you get through a piece of paper tissue spread over the top of another glass. Add more water if needed to fill up the glass. Where you live, the tapwater may be acidic or basic, and the pigment in the cabbage may turn red or blue while you are making the solution.

If you stir a few drops of lemon juice, which is acidic, into the purple solution, it will turn red. Divide the red solution equally into four glasses and stir into the solutions the following household compounds, which are bases. To the first glass, add a pinch of baking soda. To the second glass, add a pinch of washing soda. To the third glass, add a pinch of borax, and to the fourth glass, add a drop of Milk of Magnesia. Remember to wash your hands after mixing these solutions. The red solution in each glass will turn different shades of blue at different rates. You can turn the blue solutions red again by adding acids such as lemon juice or white vinegar to them. You can do this same experiment with parts of other plants to see if they contain anthocyanin. Two you might want to try are blueberries and beet roots. You may see bubbles form in the basic solutions when you add acid. These are bubbles of carbon dioxide, which you will find out more about later on in this chapter.

If you leave raspberries out at room temperature, they will turn a darker colour. You can bring back their red colour by adding a few drops of lemon juice.

BLOODSTAIN CHEMISTRY

Did you ever want to know if a red stain was blood? Polident tablets, used for cleaning false teeth, can also be used to detect and measure bloodstains. A Polident tablet contains chemicals called oxidizers, as well as blue and yellow food colouring. When the tablet is dissolved in water, the oxidizers attack the two food colourings slowly and change them into colourless products in about two hours. A trace of blood, however, acts as a catalyst on the blue colouring. This means that blood speeds up the oxidizers and causes them to destroy the blue colouring much quicker than normal. To see the effect of blood as a catalyst, try the following experiment.

Cut out a piece of paper tissue, about the size of your thumbnail. Fold the square in half twice. Cut the square into four pieces along the folds. Cut one of the smaller pieces in half again. Using a pair of tweezers, press one of the larger pieces and one of the smaller pieces against a piece of raw steak or hamburger. Use one of the other pieces as a blank. This is important if you want to show that it is the blood, and not the tissue, that is causing the chemical reaction.

Dissolve a Polident tablet in water. It will fizz and produce a clear blue-green solution. Divide the solution into three cups. You will need a clock or watch with a second hand to time the reactions. Stir the larger stained tissue into one cup and time how long it takes before you see a change in the colour of the solution. Then do the same for the smaller stained tissue and the blank, using the other two cups.

A fresh drop of blood will change the colour of the solution from blue-green to yellow in a few seconds. Smaller amounts will take longer. The blank will have no effect on the speed of the chemical reaction, so the solution should turn colourless in about two hours, just like it normally would. Try this experiment with different sizes of bloodstained tissue and try to predict how long each reaction will take. Bloodstains will speed up this chemical reaction even when they are several days old.

One of the jobs of forensic chemists who work in police laboratories is to detect blood. They don't use Polident in their tests, but they do use other substances that work in the same way to show that blood is present, even in very, very small amounts.

HYDROGEN PEROXIDE

Hydrogen peroxide is closely related to water, but it has one more oxygen atom in each molecule. A water molecule is H_2O (two hydrogen atoms and one oxygen atom), and a hydrogen peroxide molecule is H_2O_2 (two hydrogen atoms and two oxygen atoms). Hydrogen peroxide is used as a disinfectant to kill bacteria and as a bleaching agent. It can also be used as a source of oxygen.

An enzyme called catalase is present in both raw meat and raw potatoes. It is also present in blood. Catalase acts on hydrogen peroxide to convert it to oxygen and water. One molecule of catalase can bring about the breakdown of about 44,000 molecules of hydrogen peroxide in one second at 0°C (32°F). Bombardier beetles use this catalase reaction to squirt hot liquid from their abdomens at their enemies. They make oxygen gas from the hydrogen peroxide stored in special sacs in their bodies and use it in their "air guns." They can send a spray about 10 centimetres (4 inches) and the reaction happens so quickly, you can hear it go pop. In the following experiment, you will be able to see a similar reaction yourself.

The hydrogen peroxide you can buy at a drugstore is a 3% solution. Pour about 15 millilitres (1 tablespoon) of this solution into a drinking glass. Break up half a spoonful of raw hamburger into the glass. You will see a fizz of bubbles of oxygen form around each piece of meat as the catalase in the beef blood comes into contact with the hydrogen peroxide. You can see the oxygen bubbles more easily by adding a few drops of liquid soap to the glass. When the oxygen gas escapes, it will blow soap bubbles and a head of foam will appear in the glass in a few minutes. Although potatoes and turnips do not have blood, they do have catalase, and you can do the same experiment with the peeled and chopped vegetables.

In this experiment, you will also notice that the red colour of the beef blood is bleached to yellow by the hydrogen peroxide. Brunettes sometimes make themselves blonde by bleaching their hair with hydrogen peroxide. In the forest industry huge quantities of hydrogen peroxide are used to bleach the colour out of paper pulp.

BUBBLE, BUBBLE

Bubbles can form and grow in a liquid containing a dissolved gas wherever the liquid touches a sharp edge. These places are called nucleation sites, and they are present on any tiny, solid particles in the liquid or in scratches on the container walls. Small bubbles give up energy when they grow into large ones, so bubbles tend to grow until they are too big to hang on to the nucleation site. Then they let go, float to the top of the liquid, and burst.

Pop is fizzy because carbon dioxide (CO_2) is dissolved in it. To prevent nucleation and foaming in pop, manufacturers use ultraclean water that has few suspended particles. However, you can often see bubbles rising from certain places on the sides of a glass of pop. Mark the location where a bubble stream starts by drawing a circle on the outside of the glass with a wax crayon. Carefully empty the pop into another glass, wash and dry the inside of the first glass, and then pour the pop back into the glass and see where the bubble stream starts again. This may seem mysterious, but the glass does not really have a "memory." It just has a small, often invisible scratch on the inside where bubbles grow most easily (a nucleation site).

In pop that has not been shaken, any particles in the liquid will have settled to the bottom. When the container is opened, only a few bubbles escape from the scratches on the container's inside wall. Shaking a can of pop mixes

any particles throughout the pop, providing many nucleation sites. Now when the container is opened the bubbles gush out all at once in a spurt of foam.

The following experiments show the nucleation effect in a much less messy way than opening a can of shaken pop. Bubbles of carbon dioxide are much less dense

than pop, so they float to the top. Raisins are denser than pop and normally sink to the bottom. But if enough bubbles collect on them, they can be lifted to the top. Drop a few pieces of cut-up raisins into a glass of clear pop. Bubbles of carbon dioxide soon grow on the wrinkles on the raisins because they act as nucleation sites. When the raisins have collected enough large bubbles, they float up in the pop

like carbon dioxide balloons. At the top of the liquid, the bubbles burst, and the raisins sink again to get another load of bubbles. These "raisin' raisins" will dance up and down for many hours until the pop goes flat.

A more impressive way to do this is to add lots of nucleation sites all at once. Carefully pour some unshaken pop into a glass and hold it over the sink. Then add, all at once, about 15 millilitres (1 tablespoon) of table salt. The pop will froth up and right out of the glass in a spectacular burp. This happens because the sharp edges of the salt crystals provide many nucleation sites. Also, since salt water does not dissolve as much carbon dioxide as pure water, the dissolved salt forces more of the carbon dioxide out of the solution.

The naturally carbonated water of Lake Nyos in Cameroon (in central Africa) erupted in a giant "burp" in 1986, raising the water level 25 metres (82 feet) and flooding a nearby valley with carbon dioxide gas. Since this gas is 1.5 times heavier than air, it pushed the air out of the valley, and 1,700 people and all of their animals were suffocated. Chemists and geologists are studying Lake Nyos and other similar lakes to be able to warn people when such an eruption is about to occur again.

FOOD COLOURING

In 1952, A.J.P. Martin and R.L.M. Synge, two British scientists, received the Nobel Prize in chemistry for inventing a process called paper chromatography. Paper chromatography is a very powerful tool that chemists use to separate mixtures of chemicals that are found in our bodies and in plants and animals into simpler chemicals. In this experiment, you will use the same method to separate and identify the different pigments in green food colouring.

Cut a 5 x 20 centimetre (2 x 8 inch) strip of paper towel and staple the top of it to an opened-up paper clip. Lay the paper clip wire across the mouth of a 1-litre (1-quart) glass jar and let the paper strip hang down inside. Trim off the bottom of the strip so that it just about touches the bottom of the jar.

Draw a light pencil line across the strip, 2.5 cm (1 in) from the bottom, and mark off this starting line into quarters. Use a toothpick to put a tiny spot of yellow food colouring at the first quarter mark. Put a spot of green food colouring at the second quarter mark and a spot of blue food colouring at the third quarter mark. Your paper chromatogram is now loaded with food colouring chemicals and is ready for development.

To develop the chromatogram, put 60 millilitres (1/4 cup) of water in the jar and lower the chromatogram carefully so that it gets wet evenly along the bottom edge. The water will immediately

start to climb up the paper strip. When the edge of the rising water, called the solvent front, comes to the coloured spots, they will begin to move with it.

Wait about 40 minutes. By this time the solvent front will be about 10 cm (4 in) from the starting line, and the yellow and blue spots will have moved different distances. This is because the molecules of the blue food colouring are more strongly attracted to the paper than those of the yellow, so they do not climb as far.

Remove the developed chromatogram from the jar and let it dry. You will see that the original green spot in the centre lane has separated into a higher yellow spot matching the yellow spot in lane one, and into a lower blue spot matching the pure blue compound in lane three. This shows that the green food colouring is actually a mixture of yellow and blue.

Try this experiment with other food colourings to find out what you can learn about them.

6 Plants & People

Plants are the primary food source for all animal life on earth. This means that all the food people and other animals eat can be traced back to plants.

People and animals also depend on plants for the oxygen they need. They breathe in air, and the chemical factories in their cells use the oxygen in the air for their life processes. The supply of oxygen used by people and animals breathing in the air is replenished by plants.

People and animals exhale carbon dioxide, because it is a waste product they do not need.

Green plants do exactly the opposite. They use the carbon dioxide in air to make their stems, fruit, leaves, and roots, and they exhale oxygen. So the waste products of our breath help plants live, and the waste products of plants help us to survive and grow.

It takes about 75 trees to make the oxygen used by one person in a lifetime. But most of the oxygen in the environment is made by algae, an extremely large group of small plants that live in water.

SEEDS

Before farmers plant crops, they test a sample of their seeds to make sure they are alive. If most of the seeds in the sample start to grow or germinate, the farmer can be sure of getting enough plants. People sometimes do not realize that seeds that have been kept in storage are living organisms, waiting for the right conditions to grow.

During germination, a seed absorbs water and swells up until it bursts its coat. Most seeds will start to sprout in a few hours, but some will not germinate until their coats have been gnawed by animals or roasted in a fire. When a plant starts to grow, the growing tip of the root emerges first, followed by the tip of the growing shoot which will become the stem of the plant. Starch stored in the seed feeds the root and shoot until the new plant can make enough cells to make its own food.

In the kitchen, you can sprout the seeds of alfalfa, lemon, mungbean, orange, popcorn, radish, and wheat. Sprouts might also be obtained from the seeds of apple, avocado, bean, date, fig, grapefruit, hazelnut, lime, pea, peach, and prunes. Place the seeds between wet paper towels and store them in a warm, dark cupboard. Examine the seeds twice a day, write down the numbers of seeds that have sprouted, and make sure that the towels stay moist. If you like, you can carefully transplant the sprouted seeds into a flowerpot or the garden and grow your own plants. Remember, some plants won't grow outside if it's too cold.

Plants are used for fuel in many parts of the world. Also, in many places forests are burned to make room for crops. Because of these and other factors, about 400 plant species are lost forever each year. Biologists have created seed banks to save plants for future generations of people. They also hope the banked seeds could be used to create new varieties of useful plants. Banked seeds are kept in cold storage. Cold temperatures slow down the chemical reactions in seeds and let them live for a long time. The record for age before germination is held by 10,000-year-old lupine seeds dug up from frozen soil in the Canadian arctic. Possibly, unused mines in the arctic could be used as seed banks.

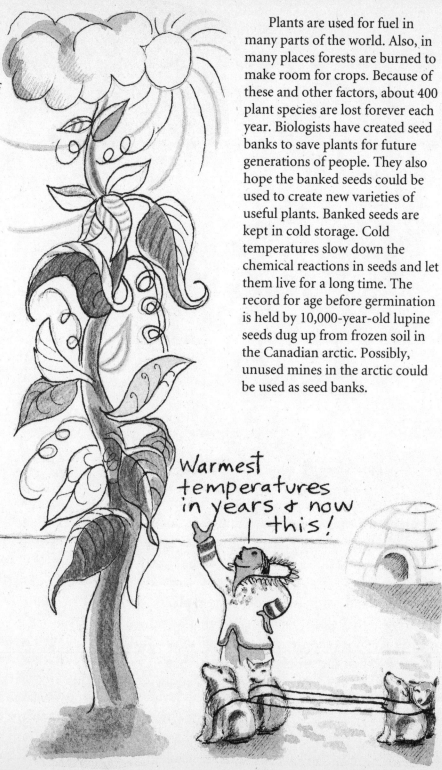

Warmest temperatures in years & now this!

BEAN SPROUTS

Mungbean sprouts are a tasty food when stir-fried or used in salads. You can buy mungbeans at food stores and use them to grow your own sprouts. You can grow sprouts in about four days.

Put 60 millilitres (1/4 cup) of beans in a wide-mouthed 1-litre (1-quart) glass jar and cover the jar with cheesecloth held in place with a rubber band. The cheesecloth will keep the beans in the jar as you pour rinse water in and out through the cheesecloth.

Soak the beans in water overnight. Then pour off the water and rinse the beans with tap water. Place the moist beans in a warm, dark cupboard to grow. Keep the jar in the dark while the sprouts are growing so they will be colourless. If they grow in the light, they turn green and have an unpleasant taste.

Rinse the beans twice a day and you will soon see a sprout growing from each bean. In about four days, when the jar is nearly full of sprouts, wash away the green seed husks. The sprouts are ready to eat. Growing plants without soil is called hydroponics and is a method proposed for feeding space travellers.

Many environmental factors can affect the growth of plants. One of these factors is water. In many places, tap water is chlorinated to kill bacteria. If you live somewhere where the water is chlorinated, try the following experiment to measure the effect of chlorinated tapwater on the growth of sprouts. Measure the same amount of mungbeans into each of two 1-litre (1-quart) glass jars. Follow the sprouting procedure using tapwater in one jar and chlorine-free, purified water in the other jar. Purified water is sold at food stores, and you will need about three litres (3 quarts) of it.

After three days, compare the volume of sprouts in each jar by filling the jars to overflowing under the tap, then pouring the water from each jar into a measuring cup. Subtract the volume of water found in each jar from the volume of the empty jar to get the sprout volume. You will find that you get more sprouts when the rinse water is not chlorinated.

At first, beans use the energy stored inside themselves to grow. But once they sprout, they need chemicals to grow. Where do the mungbeans get these chemicals? They get the carbon and oxygen they need from the 0.03% of carbon dioxide (CO_2) in the air. More oxygen and the hydrogen for the beans come from the rinse water (H_2O).

Plants also need the elements potassium, nitrogen, phosphorus, and sulphur, as well as traces of sodium, magnesium, and iron. Plants growing in soil get these elements from fertilizers and from the soil itself. The mungbeans get them from the rinse water, which has tiny but sufficient quantities dissolved in it.

I have this strange feeling—I've been eating too many sprouts!

CARROTS

Carotene is the chemical that gives carrots their colour. Carotene is also found in tomatoes, spinach, butter, eggs, leaves, and flowers. You can easily separate carotene from these materials using mineral oil that you might find in your medicine cabinet or can buy from a drugstore.

Mash 5 millilitres (1 teaspoon) of grated carrot with 10 mL (2 teaspoons) of mineral oil. Pour the mixture onto a piece of paper tissue spread over the top of a glass. After a few minutes, the solution of carotene will drip through the paper. Label this solution Sample A. Stir 5 mL (1 teaspoon) of butter with 10 mL (2 teaspoons) of mineral oil and then filter the mixture in the same way as above to get Sample B.

When you compare Samples A and B by looking at them against a piece of white paper under a strong light, they should be identical golden yellow oils with no odour or flavour.

A ripe tomato gives a mineral oil solution of carotene an orange colour rather than yellow because tomatoes also contain a red pigment called lycopene. The carotene and lycopene mix together to produce orange. A solution made from spinach will be greenish-gold from a green pigment called chlorophyll. Chlorophyll is the chemical that helps turn carbon dioxide and water into the oxygen we breathe and new plant cells for stems, leaves, and flowers. The carotene and chlorophyll blend to make the greenish-gold colour. You could do the same experiment with green leaves, and the oil solution will be similar in colour to the one from spinach.

At the end of summer, deciduous trees stop growing before they lose their leaves. Since the plant is no longer growing, it doesn't need the chlorophyll in its leaves, and the chlorophyll gets used up by the plant cells. Most leaves contain both chlorophyll and carotene in different parts of their cells. These are usually spread fairly evenly throughout the leaf. The green of chlorophyll is a very strong colour, so it hides the colour of the carotene. But without the chlorophyll to hide it, the carotene in the leaves shows up as brilliant autumn colours. If you live in a part of the country where the leaves turn colour in the fall, grind up some red or yellow leaves and repeat the same procedure as you did for carrots and butter. You will make a golden yellow solution.

Enzymes in our bodies convert carotene first into Vitamin A, and then into a chemical called visual purple inside our eyes. The visual purple molecules are light-sensitive like the photocells in the doorways of food stores, and they detect the light that we see. Now you see why you should eat your carrots, or other foods that contain carotene. But you only need a small amount. Carotene is also the basis of some sun tanning pills. If you use too many of them, your skin can turn orange.

RUBBER

In 1770, a scientist named Joseph Priestley invented the name "rubber" for the elastic material obtained from the sap of rubber trees. This milky sap, called latex, seeps out to heal the wound when the living plant is cut. Natural rubber and chewing gum are made from latex by drying it. You can make your own natural rubber from dandelions.

With a pair of scissors, snip off the ripe seed head from a dandelion while it is still growing in the ground. In a few seconds, the milky white latex will ooze up around the top of the hollow stem and you can collect it by touching it with a piece of plastic. Cut off the stem again, about one centimetre (0.4 inch) below the first cut, and collect the latex there. You can repeat the cutting and collecting all the way down the stem. Do not try to press the latex out of the stem because that will mix it with other plant juices, which will prevent rubber from forming.

Scrape the latex off the plastic and rub it into a ball between your finger and thumb. Test this dandelion rubber for elasticity by bouncing it. You will also find that you can erase pencil marks with it.

A natural rubber molecule contains thousands of carbon atoms linked together in a long, flexible chain. The molecules are stretchable and flexible, much like a coiled telephone cord, and this makes natural rubber elastic and chewable.

To make natural rubber hard, it is heated with sulphur. This process links the carbon chain molecules in nearby chains to each other with sulphur atoms. The network of carbon and sulphur atoms is harder than natural rubber, but it is still flexible and can be made into tires for cars and bicycles. This process, called vulcanization, was accidentally discovered by Charles Goodyear in 1839. Goodyear was trying to find ways to improve rubber. During one of his experiments, he dropped some rubber and sulphur onto a hot stove. It turned out to be a very fortunate accident.

Synthetic rubber is made from small molecules containing carbon and hydrogen atoms found in petroleum and natural gas. In the manufacturing process, the small molecules are linked up with each other to make long chain molecules very similar to those in natural rubber. By changing the kinds of small molecules (called "monomers"), chemists can custom build new kinds of rubbers that have different properties (harder, softer, less brittle in cold) than those of natural rubber. Synthetic rubbers are more resistant to chemical reactions than natural rubber, and are used in plumbing and for containers for storing all kinds of things.

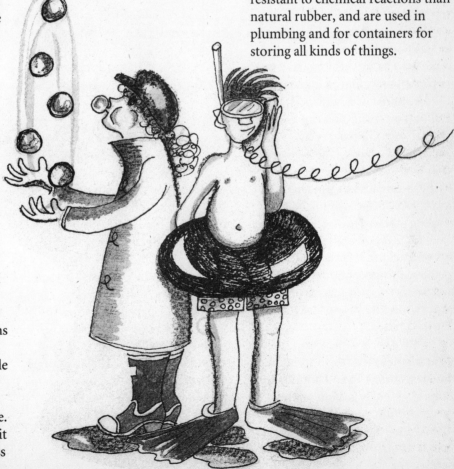

PAPER

As you read in "Rubber," small molecules can be joined together to form long chains. Nature joins together the sugar molecules called glucose (made from carbon dioxide, water, and sunlight with the help of chlorophyll) in several different ways. One of these ways makes long, strong chains called cellulose, which is the building material of all plants.

We use cellulose fibres from plants to make paper. The fibres in paper can be recycled to make new paper. By recycling 54 kilograms (120 pounds) of newspapers, one tree can be saved. You can make your own writing paper by recycling the parts of a newspaper that have no printing.

Printing presses put about 1 gram (0.04 ounce) of ink on each page of a newspaper. This ink must be removed before the paper is recycled. Since it is very hard to remove this ink at home (and ink is very messy), for this experiment you should use newspaper that has no ink on it.

Fold a sheet of newspaper lengthwise so that the unprinted borders at the top and bottom are several layers thick. Cut off the strips of unprinted paper and snip them into little pieces. Wash your hands frequently with soap and

Hey! How long's it take to get toilet paper around here?

water to keep the printer's ink from rubbing off onto the paper bits.

Blend 60 millilitres (1/4 cup) of paper bits in about 150 mL (2/3 cup) of water in a blender or food processor for a few seconds, scraping the paper pulp from the sides of the bowl with a plastic spatula. When the pulp is as thick as porridge, add 5 mL (1 teaspoon) of grated raw potato. The starch in the potato will help bind the cellulose fibres together in your paper sheet. Add another 175 mL (3/4 cup) of water slowly and

continue blending until the pulp suspension is smooth and creamy and free from lumps.

Lay a piece of plastic window screen (available at hardware stores) over a muffin pan. Pour the wet paper pulp onto the screen, spreading it with a spatula into a letter-sized layer. Cover the wet pulp with a second piece of screen and gently press the screens together, squishing the water out. When most of the water has drained off, lift the two screens off the pan and place them on a towel. Lift the top screen and repair any holes in the pulp with the spatula. Cover the top screen with another towel and roll the paper sheet with a rolling pin until it is strong enough to be lifted from the screen.

Dry the paper in a microwave oven for about 1 minute on the high setting. Roll it again while it is still warm. Newsprint paper is made in a continuous roll with a machine that spreads and dries the pulp on belts of screen with rollers. The paper sheet is heated with steam instead of microwaves.

Your paper is now ready for trimming. This kind of paper is useful for notes and cards, since it is thicker than most of the paper you use.

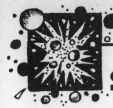

STARCH

Many animals can run across quicksand as if it were solid ground, but if they stop, the quicksand turns to liquid and they sink. A mixture of cornstarch and water also has this unusual behaviour of changing from liquid to solid and back again depending on how quickly it is stirred. Many substances will turn from liquid to solid when pressure is applied, and you can observe this in the following experiment.

Put about 15 millilitres (1 tablespoon) of cornstarch powder in an egg cup and add 5 mL (1 teaspoon) of water a little at a time as you stir the starch slowly. The mixture will become thick and creamy. Now stir the starch and water mixture quickly, and it will become solid. Stop stirring, and the mixture will become liquid again. You may have to experiment with the ratios of cornstarch and water until you get the mixture that works the best.

Try pushing your finger into the mixture quickly and then slowly. When you push quickly, the mixture feels solid and resists you, but when you push slowly, your finger will go right to the bottom of the egg cup. If you try to pull your finger out quickly, you will lift up the egg cup. Pour the mixture into your hand and roll it into a ball with your other hand. The mixture will stay firm while you are doing this. Stop rolling the ball, and it will melt and run through your fingers.

Molecules of starch are chains of many thousands of smaller ring molecules of glucose ($C_6H_{12}O_6$). Each glucose ring has atoms of oxygen attached to it. Each oxygen atom carries a hydrogen atom. Water (H_2O) also has oxygen and hydrogen groups. OH groups in the starch strongly attract the OH groups in the water. When you stir the starch and water slowly, the water molecules have time to push in between the starch molecules and the mixture stays liquid. When you stir the mixture quickly, the water is pushed aside, and starch molecules line up and bond together to form a solid jelly-like substance. When you stop stirring, the water molecules move in quickly and the mixture dissolves again into a liquid.

Plants make glucose from carbon dioxide, water, and solar energy through a process called photosynthesis. They store some of the glucose as starch. When animals eat plants, the enzymes in their bodies separate the starch into glucose units, and their blood carries it to their cells. There the solar energy stored in the glucose molecules is released to provide energy. The carbon dioxide and water from the glucose molecules are released as waste products.

So I say, slow down and enjoy life!

CATNIP

Some animals are strongly attracted to chemicals in certain plants. The giant panda bears of China will eat only bamboo shoots, and the koalas of Australia eat only the leaves of the eucalyptus tree. Most cats are strongly attracted to catnip, the leaves of the *nepeta cataria* plant.

You can buy catnip at the pet store or grow your own to make a catnip mouse for your cat. The mouse can be made from a roll of cloth. Sew the edges of the roll together so it won't unravel and tie it with string in the shape of a mouse. You can add a string for a tail.

Put crushed fresh catnip leaves or dried catnip in a freezer bag along with the cloth. Close the bag, shake it, and leave it sealed for 24 hours. The catnip chemical called

nepetalactone will slowly seep out of the leaves and into the cloth mouse. When you take the cloth out of the freezer bag, brush the nepeta leaves back into the bag and seal it again to be ready for another treatment. Now give the toy to your cat and it will have a wonderful time.

Cats might toss the toy, chase it, lie on it, drool over it, and sleep on it. The nepetalactone on the toy will not harm rugs or furniture or bother people or dogs since they cannot smell it. The chemical detectors in the cat's body that detect the odour of catnip must be different from those in the bodies of people and dogs.

After a day or so, the nepetalactone will evaporate from the cloth, and you can return the toy mouse to the plastic bag for

another treatment. You might make two toys so that one could be kept in the catnip container while the cat has the other one, and they could be exchanged every few days.

A cat's response to catnip is inherited, and some cats aren't interested at all. Their response does not depend on whether the cat is male or female or whether it is neutered. Older cats usually play less enthusiastically than younger cats and are likely to go to sleep with the toy mouse.

Nepetalactone belongs to the family of chemical compounds called esters, which include the odour chemicals of banana, apple, and pineapple. We enjoy the odours while we eat the fruit, but are not usually as crazy for them as cats are for their catnip.

ONIONS

Onions, garlic, chives, shallots, and leeks are bulbs of plants that belong to the lily family. They all have strong odours that make them interesting as foods and flavourings. If we could not smell them, they would all taste bland.

Some cookbooks suggest that one way to remove onion odour from your breath is to chew fresh parsley. The green chlorophyll in the parsley is thought to react with the onion odour. If this is so, then chewing fresh spinach, which has lots of chlorophyll, should be equally effective in curing onion-breath.

Why don't you try an onion-breath experiment with the help of some friends? After eating onion some of you could try parsley and some could try spinach. Judges could then smell all your breaths to see if they can detect onions. Remember that anyone who tastes onion will have their onion-odour-detector overloaded and will not be able to smell onion on someone else's breath. So the judges will have to be onion-free.

Freshly cut onions release gaseous chemical compounds containing sulphur that can get into your eyes and make you cry. These are natural tear gases called "lachrimators," and they dissolve easily in water. To peel an onion without tears, hold it under the tap and let a stream of water run over it as you cut.

You can remove onion odour from your hands by rubbing them with a piece of lemon. The lemon juice contains vitamin C that reacts with the sulphur compounds in the onion to change them to odourless compounds.

The chief chemical compound in oil of garlic also contains sulphur. It has a very strong odour that lasts longer than the onion odour, but it is not a tear-jerker. As with onions, the best way to protect yourself from the odour of garlic on someone else's breath is to eat garlic yourself.

Onions and garlic have long been supposed to help cure everything from colds to wounds. Since it is only the freshly-cut bulbs that are believed to be effective, the treatment requires constantly changing the supply, and the strong odours and tears could be unpleasant for both the patient and the healer. So far the effectiveness of the treatments seems to be uncertain.

7 Food Chemistry

We are what we eat. Our bodies are efficient chemical factories that transform the food we eat every day into the energy we need to live and work and play. These processes involve chemical changes. New compounds are formed from other ones, sometimes in simple processes and other times in very complex ways. To understand how food works in our bodies, we need to understand the chemistry of food itself.

In a way, we might say that chemistry started with the discovery of cooking by prehistoric people. Near the fossil skeleton of a woman found in a cave near Beijing, China were wood ashes and some cooked animal bones. Chemists measured the radiation in and around the bones and showed that they were 225,000 years old, the oldest cooked bones ever found.

When meat is cooked, chemical reactions change the meat. These changes help preserve the meat so it can be kept longer than fresh meat. So the first "chemist" who cooked meat made life easier for the rest of the people around.

 **BUTTER**

Butter is made nearly everywhere in the world. In some countries, people make butter from the milk of goats, sheep, and horses. Most of our butter comes from cow's milk. When butter is heated, it forms a clear, thin liquid called ghee. It keeps better than butter and is used in places with hot climates.

Half-fill a screw-capped jar with cool whipping cream (the liquid, not the kind in spray cans). Put the lid on the jar and rock it end-to-end. In about 10 minutes, the sloshing sound of the cream will change to a thud. This means that a lump of butter has formed. Continue rocking the jar back and forth. When no more butter will form, pour off the liquid.

Wash the butter by pouring ice water into the jar and rocking it again. Discard the milky wash water and transfer the butter to a bowl. Add cool water and press the butter with a spoon. Carefully pour off the wash water. Repeat the process until the wash water is clear.

Press out the last traces of water from the butter then mix in a tiny amount of salt to make the butter taste better. This is one experiment result that you can eat!

Carotene (see "Carrots") is in the grasses and other plants that cows eat. It is the carotene in a cow's food that gives butter its yellow colour. Margarine is made from purified plant oils and is colourless. Carotene or other plant colours are often added to margarine to make it look like butter.

EGG QUESTIONS

Do you know how to tell if an egg is fresh? Why do yolks sometimes turn green in a boiled egg? Here are some experiments that might answer some of your egg questions.

1. How can you tell if an egg is cooked?

Spin an uncooked egg in the centre of your kitchen table and note the time it takes for the egg to come to a stop. Do the same with a hard-boiled egg. A hard-boiled egg will spin nearly twice as long as an uncooked egg. There is a theory that the motion of the liquid in the raw egg takes up—absorbs—some of the energy and slows down the rotation. If the theory is correct, a water-filled egg should slow the spin even more because water moves more easily than raw egg. Therefore the water should absorb more of the spinning egg's energy.

To test this theory poke a small hole in each end of a raw egg with a needle. Stir the egg inside the shell with the needle to break the yolk. Then blow the liquid egg out into a bowl. (This may take quite a long time.) Seal up one hole with household glue or a small piece of tape or chewed gum. Place the egg under a tap and fill it with water. Then seal the open end. Now compare the spin time of your "water egg" with the spin times of raw and cooked eggs.

2. How does an egg breathe?

Eggs are laid by birds and some other animals. The young animals develop inside the egg and need air to grow. Air enters the egg through tiny holes in the shell called pores.

Soak a raw egg in grape juice, then rinse it off and crack the egg. Inside the shell you will see coloured spots where the pores have let in the juice.

3. Can you tell how fresh an egg is?

Dissolve 10 millilitres (2 teaspoons) of table salt in about 150 mL (2/3 cup) of water in a glass measuring cup. Place a fresh egg in the solution, then an older

egg. (Check the "best before" date on the egg carton to find out how old an egg is.) A fresh egg will sink to the bottom of the salt solution and lie on its side. A two- to three-day-old egg will float just below the liquid surface with the big end slightly higher than the small end. As the egg gets older the big end rises more and more.

Eggs float because they breathe in air. The big end of an egg has an air space where the air collects that comes in through the pores. As an egg gets older, it has more time to breathe, and more air collects in the big end. The more air in the egg, the less dense the egg becomes, and the higher it floats in the water.

4. How can you prevent green yolks in boiled eggs?

You may have seen a hard-boiled egg with a green yolk. Although it is still good to eat, some people don't like the way it looks. The protein in egg contains sulphur and hydrogen. As an egg is warmed, some of the sulphur and hydrogen react to form hydrogen sulphide (H_2S). When the egg cools slowly, the hydrogen sulphide reacts with the iron in the yolk to form green iron sulphide (FeS).

To see this for yourself, boil two eggs for 7 minutes. Remove one egg and quickly cool it under cold water. Let the other egg slowly cool in the hot water. When both are cool, open them up. The egg cooled quickly will have a yellow yolk because it cooled quickly and iron sulphide did not have time to form.

sob! I can't go in until I'm a little older...

MICROORGANISMS

Very small plants and animals that can be seen only under a microscope are called microorganisms. These include bacteria, yeasts, and moulds. Since ancient times, people have used microorganisms for making bread, sauerkraut, cheese, tea, wine, beer, vinegar, and yogurt. Modern chemists use microorganisms to help them manufacture food, drugs, and valuable chemicals.

Bacteria are the youngest form of life because they produce a new generation in about 20 minutes. They are also the oldest because they have been on earth for about 3.6 billion years. Most of them are so small that it would take 1,000 of them lined up side by side to measure one millimetre (0.04 inch). They are found on glaciers, in hot springs deep under the sea, and inside and on our bodies where most are helpful to us, but a few can make us sick.

You can use bacteria to make your own yogurt. You will need a starter sample of the bacteria *Lactobacillus bulgaricus*, which are in the yogurt you can buy at a food

store. Warm a glass of low-fat milk in a pot or microwave oven. It is important that the milk is just warm. If it is hot, the experiment won't work, because the heat will kill the bacteria when you add them. Put the warm milk in a glass and stir in about 30-45 millilitres (2-3 tablespoons) of plain yogurt. Cover the glass with plastic wrap, wrap the glass in a towel to keep it warm, and place it in a cardboard box. In about three hours, you will have a glass of yogurt, which should then be refrigerated. When you are ready to eat your yogurt, you might like to add some fresh fruit or jam to make it more tasty. But remember to save some of the plain yogurt for starting your next batch.

You might even have a yogurt maker at home. Yogurt makers have a heater that keeps the mixture at just the right temperature for the bacteria to grow.

Certain complicated molecules that are too expensive to manufacture are made by some microorganisms as part of their life cycle. To make the drug penicillin, for example, chemists first grow a mould by feeding it simple starting materials like sugar and water. Then the mould is harvested, and the complicated product molecules separated out. Chemists convert these product compounds into penicillin, which doctors use to treat diseases.

BAKING AND FERMENTATION

The same chemical reaction that changes grape juice to wine also helps to make bread dough rise. In each case, a sugar called glucose is transformed by a process called fermentation into alcohol, carbon dioxide gas, and energy. This reaction is caused by tiny amounts of chemicals called enzymes, which are found in the living cells of the grapes and of the yeast in the dough.

Glucose is sold in food stores as corn syrup, and you can ferment it in a plastic cup. Stir about 2.5 millilitres (1/2 teaspoon) of corn syrup with 7.5 mL (1/2 tablespoon) of warm water and add a pinch of fresh baker's yeast. Place the cup in a warm place—by a sunny window or a fireplace—for 30 minutes. You can also place the cup in a bowl partly filled with warm water. Do not use too much water or it will overflow. By the end of that time, you should be able to see bubbles of gas rising in the liquid and smell the yeasty odour of fresh bread. The bubbles are carbon dioxide that make the froth on beer and champagne and make bread dough rise.

A similar chemical reaction happens with glucose inside our bodies. Glucose is carried by your blood to your body cells. There it is converted into energy and carbon dioxide by enzymes. You use the energy produced to work and play. The carbon dioxide produced is carried to your lungs by your blood, and you breathe it out into the air. Plants absorb the carbon dioxide you breathe out and use it to make glucose to start the cycle all over again.

CURDS AND WHEY

Cheese-making is older than recorded history. Cheese is made from casein, a protein found in milk. When treated with an acid or a chemical called an enzyme, casein forms solid clots, called curds. The rest of the milk, which is mostly water, is called whey. In a cheese factory, the curds and whey are put into cheesecloth bags. The bags are put through powerful presses, to separate the curds and whey. The curds are cured with heat or bacteria to produce different kinds of cheeses that can be hard or soft, strong or mild. Cheese is made from the milk of many different animals: cows, goats, sheep, camels. Each cheese has its own distinctive flavour and odour.

To make a cheese "dessert," you need rennet tablets. These can be found in the pudding section of your grocery store, under the trade name Junket.

Put 250 millilitres (1 cup) of milk in a bowl, and add 25 mL (2 tablespoons) of sugar and 2.5 mL (1/2 teaspoon) of vanilla or other flavouring. Heat the solution in the top of a double boiler and stir until it is lukewarm or about 43°C (110 °F). Crush a rennet tablet in 5 mL (1 teaspoon) of warm water, add the mixture to the milk, and *stir for a few seconds only.* Quickly pour the dessert into two dishes.

Let the dessert stand at room temperature undisturbed for 10 minutes. It will start to solidify during this time. To prevent the separation of the curds and the whey, place the dishes in the refrigerator as soon as the 10 minutes is up. After 20 minutes in the fridge, your cheese dessert will be ready to eat.

Whole milk is 87% water, 5% carbohydrates, 4% fat, 3% protein, and 1% minerals. The enzyme called rennin in the rennet tablet reacts with part of the milk protein (casein) and allows the rest of the casein to form solid clots (curds). These clots entangle the milk fat molecules in them, but leave behind the water, carbohydrates, minerals, and other proteins (whey). But by cooling the mixture like you did here, the curds and whey don't separate.

To make separate curds, put 25 mL (2 tablespoons) of skim milk in a glass and add 10 mL (2 teaspoons) of white vinegar. Place the glass in a pot of hot water and stir the mixture while it warms. When lumps of curd appear, remove the glass from the hot water and continue stirring until the curds stop growing.

Let the mixture stand until the curds have settled out. Then filter off the liquid whey through a piece of paper tissue. Spread the moist tissue on paper towels to soak up most of the whey, then return the curds to the glass. Wash the curds by stirring them in 10 mL (2 teaspoons) of water. Filter off the wash water through fresh paper tissue. Continue washing and filtering until the curds of casein are colourless and odourless.

This casein is fun to play with, but not much fun to eat. (It is tasteless.) The moist casein can be moulded like modelling clay and imprinted with coins and other patterns. It dries and hardens to a tough solid.

Some people eat casein because it is a good source of protein. A similar casein is obtained from beans and nuts. Besides being a food, casein can be turned into a plastic by mixing it with a chemical called formaldehyde. This plastic is used for tool handles and hammer heads because it is extremely hard and durable.

ROCK CANDY

The chemical name for table sugar is sucrose. It is made from the juice of sugar cane or sugar beets. First, the juice is squeezed out of the cane or sugar beet. Then it is purified, and the extra water is evaporated until a syrup forms. The syrup slowly crystallizes until it becomes granulated sugar.

To grow your own sucrose crystals, called rock candy, stir two and a half parts of sugar into one part of hot water and set the syrup aside. In a few days, collect the glittering rock candy crystals with a spoon. Quickly wash them with a little cold water to remove the sticky syrup and let them dry. They are sweet to suck but do not try to chew them. They are so hard you might chip a tooth or crack a filling.

Canadians eat about equal amounts of beet sugar and cane sugar, which are identical in taste and appearance. This is because they are both sucrose. It takes a chemist to tell them apart. Carbon atoms are a mixture of two different varieties (isotopes) of atoms that have different weights—carbon thirteen (^{13}C) and carbon-twelve (^{12}C). The only difference between these two carbon atoms is their mass.

Using a machine called a mass spectrometer, chemists can break up the sucrose molecules and measure the weight of the atoms. The sucrose from beets has only one half as many of the heavy carbon atoms as the sucrose from sugar cane.

Maple sugar is also mainly sucrose and is made by boiling down the sap of maple trees. The maple flavour and colour are formed from compounds in the sap when it is heated. The sucrose of maple sugar, like beet sucrose, has fewer heavy carbon atoms than cane sucrose. So chemists can tell whether a sample of maple syrup is really pure or if it has been sweetened and extended with less expensive sucrose.

TEA

Tea leaves grow on camellia trees in Asia. The leaves are picked and dried to make green tea, or they are fermented before drying to make black tea. To make tea to drink, the dried leaves are steeped in hot water for about three minutes for weak tea and for about five minutes for strong tea.

In addition to water, a cup of tea contains about 0.026 % caffeine and 0.052 % tannic acid, as well as traces of chemicals that give tea colour, odour, and flavour. The amount of caffeine and tannic acid in a cup of tea increases with the time of steeping.

Tanning is a process used to make leather last longer. In this process, tannic acid is used. This tannic acid comes from the bark and wood of many different trees, but is similar to the tannic acid in tea. Tannic acid combines with the protein in the animal skin and produces a mixture poisonous to the microorganisms found there. These microorganisms would normally eat the leather, but the mixture kills them and the leather will last longer.

You can make "egg leather" by tanning egg white protein with the tannic acid in a cup of tea. Stir 5 millilitres (1 teaspoon) of egg white into a cup of cool, strong tea. In a few minutes, clots of egg leather will settle out. Let the egg white and tea mixture stand for about two hours, then filter it through paper tissue. The rust-coloured egg leather will stick to the paper, and will feel smooth and flexible when it dries. It will keep indefinitely without spoiling.

Tannic acid combines with proteins in your mouth causing them to pucker or contract. This creates the sensation called an "astringent taste" when we drink tea. Doctors sometimes use stronger solutions of tannic acid to pucker and close a wound to stop bleeding.

Ol' Eggboots burst into the saloon...

BROWN APPLES

Bananas and apples quickly turn brown when they are cut or bruised. Here is an easy way you can stop this browning reaction.

Cut a slice of apple into quarters and rub one of the quarters on a slice of lemon. Fit the quarters back together. In a few minutes, the three apple quarters that were not rubbed with lemon will turn brown, but the lemon-treated quarter will look as fresh as when you first cut the apple. The difference in the colour of the slices will last many hours.

In the first step of this browning reaction, the oxygen of the air combines with hydrogen atoms in a compound in the apple. This reaction is helped by a chemical called an enzyme, and it produces the brown coating on the apple. The citric acid in the lemon juice stops the chemical activity of the enzyme so the lemon-rubbed apple quarter does not turn brown. Citric acid can also prevent other fruits from browning, so remember to squeeze a little lemon juice over a fruit salad to keep it looking fresh.

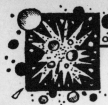

THE SOUNDS OF FOOD

A finger snap lasts for about one thousandth of a second, but you can still hear the sound it makes. The "snap" is a sonic boom made by the molecules of air rushing into the empty space created between the finger surfaces. You can also hear sonic booms made by airplanes travelling faster than sound, or lightning strikes, or huge explosions. Ultrasound is a very-high frequency sound that you can't hear, but dogs can. It is used in medicine to examine people and in chemistry, where it speeds up some reactions.

The crunching sounds you hear if you walk on spilled salt or sugar are caused by the vibrations given off by the breaking crystals. Salt and sugar crystals are made of different chemicals, and each produces its own particular sound—just as different people have different voices. You can record the sounds of foods with a tape recorder and have fun playing them for your friends.

Put a small spoonful of sugar into a long envelope and seal it. Tap the long edge of the envelope on the table to distribute the crystals in a row. Now place the envelope flat on the table and roll it with a rolling pin while you record the "big crunch" sound. The paper envelope amplifies the sound and makes it much louder than it would be if you rolled the sugar by itself or in a plastic bag.

Try the same thing with other dry household chemicals like salt and breakfast cereals and compare the sounds you hear. Record the cracking sound that ice cubes make when you drop them into a glass of water. The shattering sounds from breaking glass and ice are similar but the ice breaks into pieces with straight sides while glass pieces have curved edges. This is because ice is a crystal with orderly rows of water molecules while glass is a thick liquid of jumbled molecules of silicon dioxide.

Many dry breakfast cereals are mostly starch. They make sounds like "snap, crackle and pop" when they are suddenly wetted. Record the sounds different cereals make when you pour milk on them to see if they all sound the same. Other chemical sounds can be made by clinking metals, crushing wrappers, scratching surfaces, and tearing fabrics.

8   Body Basics

As babies we found our fingers and our toes. Then we reached out further to our mothers' faces, and on and on to all the world around us. Scientists continue this search by exploring and studying everything in the universe. It is natural for us to connect new discoveries with ourselves. To each of us the most important thing is our own body, the only one we will ever have. We can understand and care for it better if we know about its chemistry.

Our bodies are made from atoms of different elements. To understand what atoms are in your body, and how much there is of each one, imagine that they were separated and collected in different parts of your body. Since 63% of your body's atoms are hydrogen atoms, they would fill you from your toes to the bottom of your chest. The collected oxygen atoms (25.5% of the atoms) would fill you from the bottom of your chest to the top of your shoulders. Your head, your left arm, and your right arm down to the elbow would contain the carbon atoms (9.5%). Your right arm from your elbow to your wrist would be filled with nitrogen atoms (1.4%). So far, just four kinds of atoms—carbon, hydrogen, oxygen, and nitrogen—account for 99.4% of all of the atoms in your body.

The remaining 0.6% of your body's atoms are calcium atoms, enough to fill your wrist and the upper half of your right hand; phosphorus atoms to fill the lower half of the hand; potassium atoms to fill the thumb; chlorine atoms to fill the index finger; sulphur atoms to fill the ring finger; and magnesium atoms to fill the little finger down to the first joint. Iron atoms would fill up the rest of the little finger except for the fingernail, which would hold the iodine atoms.

Of course, your body's atoms are not stored separately but are joined together in many different ways to make millions of compounds. Different compounds make up muscle, bones, teeth, blood, and the other parts for your body.

Everything that we are is chemistry, and chemistry is always at work in our bodies. Even our thoughts and memories are stored and processed in our brains using chemical reactions.

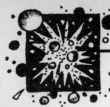

BODY DENSITY

Why will some objects float in water while others sink? The answer to this has to do with the density of the object. Density is equal to the mass of the object (how much matter it has) divided by its volume (how much space it takes up). If an object is less dense than water, it will float. If it is more dense, it will sink.

The Greek mathematician Archimedes (287-212 BC) was asked to find out whether a king's crown was pure gold or a mixture of silver and gold, without destroying it. The way to answer this question came to him while he was bathing at a public bath. The story says he was so excited that he ran home through the streets without his clothes, shouting "Eureka," which in Greek means "I have found it."

Archimedes weighed the crown to find out its mass (on earth, weight and mass are the same). Then he put it into a container that was completely full of water. A volume of water overflowed that was equal to the volume of the crown. He measured this volume by removing the crown from the container and measuring water back into the container until it was full again. Now he knew both the mass and volume of the crown and could calculate its density.

Since the density of gold is about twice that of silver, a mixture of the two would have a density less than that of pure gold. The legend does not tell us the actual

density of the crown, so we don't know if it was pure gold or not.

You can measure your body density using Archimedes' method. First, weigh yourself in kilograms (or pounds). Then fill a bathtub about one-third full of water. Lie down in the tub, and have a helper fill the tub with more water until you are completely covered except for your face. Ask your helper to mark the water level with a piece of tape. Stand up, let the water drain off, and get out of the tub. Using a large (1- or 2-litre or quart container), add water to the tub until the water level reaches the tape. On a piece of paper, keep track of the number of litres (or quarts) it takes. This is your body's volume. To find your body's density, divide your mass by your volume.

Water has a density of 1 kilogram per litre (2.1 pounds/U.S. quart). The soft tissues of our bodies are mainly water, fat, and protein. These tissues contain the chemical elements hydrogen, carbon, oxygen, and nitrogen. Each of these elements has a density less than 1 kg/L (2.1 lbs/qt). Our bones also contain the heavier elements calcium and phosphorus, which have densities of 2 to 3 kg/L (2 to 3 lbs/qt). So if you sink in water, you can blame it on your bones.

For each person, body density increases from birth to adulthood and then decreases in old age. At any age females with an average density of 1.04 kg/L (2.17 lbs/U.S. quart) are less dense than males with an average density of 1.06 kg/L (2.21 lbs/ U.S. qt).

You can amaze your friends by

using density to tell the difference between cans of diet pop and regular pop without looking at the labels or opening the cans. You can even do it in the dark.

Ask a friend to cover the labels on an unopened can of diet pop and one of regular pop. Then put the cans in a pail of water. The diet pop will float, but the can of regular pop will sink.

Regular pop contains sugar, so it is more dense than water and a can of it will sink. Diet pop contains Aspartame, which is about 160 times sweeter than sugar. The amount of Aspartame added to pop to make it sweet is so small that it gives diet pop about the same density as water. So a can of diet pop will float.

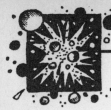

A BREATH OF AIR

When you are resting, you breathe in about half a litre (30 cubic inches) of air every four seconds. In a whole lifetime, you would breathe about 300,000 cubic metres (10 million cubic feet) of air or enough to fill a hockey arena. Your body cells need the oxygen in air to help them release the energy your body needs for work and play.

Your total lung capacity for air is related to your physical fitness. When you exercise, you breathe in much more air and more often. The more physically fit you are, the greater your lung capacity will be. The more air you take in with each breath, the more energy you will have available for your body cells.

To measure your lung capacity, get a plastic bag and check to see that there are no holes in it. Then flatten it to make sure there is no air inside. Take several deep breaths, then blow all the air you can into the plastic bag in one breath only. Seal the bag of exhaled air with a twist-tie.

Put a pail in the sink and fill it with lukewarm water until the water overflows. Press the bag of breath into the pail with a flat cover until no more water overflows. Remove

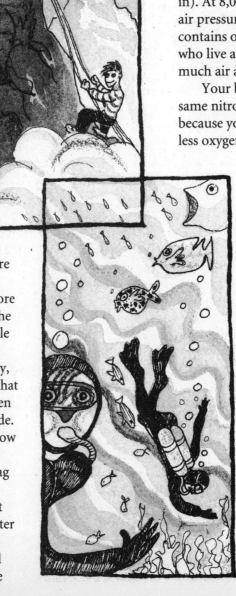

the cover and the bag and use a measuring cup to measure water back into the pail until it is just ready to overflow again. The volume of water you measured is your total lung capacity.

An average adult has a lung capacity of about 3.6 litres (220 cubic inches). People who live high in the mountains have larger lungs. This is because at sea level, air pressure is about one kilogram per square centimetre (14.2 lb/sq. in). At 8,000 metres (5 miles) above sea level, the air pressure is about half as much, and the air contains only half as much oxygen. So people who live at this altitude must breathe twice as much air as those who live by the sea.

Your breath in the plastic bag contains the same nitrogen and argon that you breathed in because your body doesn't use them. But it has less oxygen, more water vapour, and about 100 times more carbon dioxide. This is because we also breathe out waste carbon dioxide produced by our bodies. In each minute, you use about 250 millilitres (15 cubic inches) of oxygen, and you breathe out about 200 mL (12 cubic inches) of carbon dioxide. You also breathe out eight times more water vapour than you breathe in. This warm breath carries away some of our body heat, and along with perspiring, helps keep our body temperature at 37°C (98.6°F).

Deep sea divers and space travellers study the chemistry of air carefully because they must carry their atmosphere with them in steel tanks and recycle it. Their tanks also contain chemicals that will react with the carbon dioxide they exhale to keep it at a safe level.

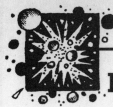

BEAUTIFUL SKIN

Our skin is a chemical wrapping that protects our bodies from harm. It helps keep our body temperature steady and destroys harmful bacteria. It absorbs ultraviolet light from the sun and uses it to convert chemicals in our body into vitamin D. We need vitamin D to help make bones and teeth, and keep

them healthy and strong. Since water and oil don't mix, our skin contains fat to keep out harmful substances dissolved in water, and water to keep out harmful substances dissolved in oil. Our skin is constantly growing from the inside and peeling off from the outside. We can see this when our skin is recovering from a sunburn or a wound.

The chemical energy that your body needs from food is related to the area of your skin. You need about twice as much energy per minute per unit of skin when you are playing than when you are sleeping.

How much skin do you have? To find out you can use the "Rule of Nines" invented by doctors to estimate how much skin has been damaged by burns. According to this rule, each arm and hand together have 9% of the total skin area, and each leg and foot together have18%.

To measure the area of the skin

on your arm, imagine that it is laid out in a flat sheet. The length of the sheet is the distance from your wrist to your shoulder, and the average width of the sheet is the distance around your arm at the elbow. Measure these two distances and multiply them to get the area of your arm. To get the area of your hand, trace it on paper ruled in squares. Count the squares your hand covers, multiply by the area of one square, and then multiply by 2 to get the area of the skin on the front and back of your hand. Now add the hand and arm areas and divide by 9. Since each hand and arm together is about 9% of your skin area, this calculation gives you the area of 1% of your skin. Multiply this number by 100 and you will get an estimate of the total area of your skin in square metres (square yards). Adults have skin areas of 15,000-20,0000 square centimetres (2,300-3,100 square inches) and the skin may weigh from 2.7 to 4.5 kilograms (6-10 pounds).

Sir Peter Medawar was an English biologist who received the Nobel Prize for medicine in 1960. He made important discoveries that helped us develop a way to transplant skin from healthy people to cover the wounds of burned patients.

GOOD BONES

There are 206 bones in our bodies, and when we are fully grown they weigh about nine kilograms (20 pounds). Bones hold our bodies upright and protect our brains and other organs. Red and white blood cells are produced in the marrow, the soft inner part of our bones.

Bones are tough because they contain a substance called collagen. Collagen is similar to silk and has long, strong, flexible molecules.

The hardness of bones comes from crystals of the mineral calcium hydroxide phosphate. This mineral contains atoms of calcium, phosphorus, oxygen, and hydrogen. You can make a bone rubbery by soaking it in acid. The process is called decalcification because it dissolves the calcium and phosphorus from the bone and leaves only the flexible collagen. If you soak a cooked chicken leg bone in vinegar for two or three days and then rinse off the vinegar, you will find you can easily bend the bone without breaking it.

The bones of space travellers undergo decalcification unless they exercise. In zero gravity, bones do not have the weight of a body to support, and so they do not need the mineral crystals to make them hard. The other parts of the body compete for the calcium and phosphorus that are not being used in the bones, and the bones get a little rubbery. When space travellers exercise, their bones stay hard and keep their calcium and phosphorus.

Bones and teeth last for millions of years and help us to understand our history. The collagen in bones contains two kinds of carbon atoms—carbon-thirteen (^{13}C) and carbon-twelve (^{12}C). The only difference between these two carbon atoms is their mass. They both react the same way chemically. People who eat grass plants like wheat and rice have more ^{13}C atoms than people who eat broad-leafed plants like potatoes and beans. Chemists and archæologists can measure the amount of ^{13}C atoms in fossil bones to learn about the diet and migrations of prehistoric people.

okay, who's the wise guy?

TRIM FINGERNAILS

Fingernails grow about 3.8 centimetres (1.5 inches) each year but toenails grow only about half as fast. Thumbnails seem to grow faster than the nails on other fingers—perhaps because thumbs are more active than fingers. This may also account for differences in growth rates between the nails of your left and right hands.

To find out the growth rate of your nails, wait until they are long enough to cut. Then cut each nail square across the centre of each nail. (You may want to file the sides of each nail after you cut them.) Wait two weeks and cut your nails again in the same way. This time save each nail clipping in a labelled envelope. Repeat the nail clipping in two weeks. Line up the two pieces

of nail from each finger and thumb so they are touching in the direction they grew. Measure the total length for each and multiply by 13. Now you have an estimate of how long each nail will grow in a year.

Fingernails are made of the protein keratin. Keratin molecules are long chains, like a bracelet. These molecules are twisted together in threes like the strands of a rope. The strands are held together by chemical bonds between sulphur atoms on the neighbouring molecular strands.

These sulphur-sulphur bonds act like glue to keep the strands together in a three-dimensional network that makes the fingernail tough and flexible.

When keratin is heated or hit sharply, the sulphur-sulphur bonds break, leaving a single electron on each sulphur atom. Single electrons behaving like tiny magnets can be detected in an instrument called an electron spin resonance (ESR) spectrometer. ESR signals from fingernail clippings show that cutting your nails breaks some of the sulphur-sulphur bonds.

BLOOD CHEMISTRY

In your lifetime, your heart will beat about 2.5 billion times to pump blood to all parts of your body. Blood moves through vessels or tubes called veins and arteries. In your lungs, the blood takes up oxygen and turns red. The red blood flows back to your heart and is pumped out again through the arteries. It flows to all your body tissues where the oxygen is used to make energy for movement and growth.

In your body tissues, the blood picks up carbon dioxide, which gives it a bluish colour. This blood then returns to your heart through the veins. The heart pumps the bluish blood to the lungs where it gives up the carbon dioxide to be breathed out. Blood picks up oxygen, turns red again, and starts the cycle once more. You can see bluish blood in the veins of your wrist and red blood on the inside of your lips.

Red blood cells are the part of the blood responsible for transporting oxygen throughout the body and getting rid of carbon dioxide. These blood cells have molecules of hæmoglobin. Hæmoglobin molecules contain iron atoms. The iron atoms pick up oxygen in the lungs. But the bond holding the iron atoms and oxygen together is very weak, so the oxygen is easily given up to the body cells. The same iron atoms then pick up carbon dioxide and release it in the lungs.

There is about three grams (0.1 ounce) of iron in our blood, and it is recycled when our red cells die. We need to eat only about 1 milligram (0.000035 ounce) of iron every day in our food to make up for any losses. A milligram of iron is just a little bigger than the period at the end of this sentence.

To see blood change from bluish to red, make a cut in a raw beefsteak. Inside the steak the beef blood is bluish because the oxygen has been used up by the tissues. However, when the cut is exposed to the air for a few minutes, the beef turns red as the blood takes up oxygen from the air.

When we are bruised, blood seeps into the damaged tissues and turns blue. The red blood cells are broken up, and the iron atoms from the hæmoglobin are recycled back into our bodies. This breakdown of hæmoglobin produces bilirubin, a yellow compound. Bilirubin makes the bruise look yellow. Eventually, the bilirubin is eliminated through our urine when the damaged tissue is healed.

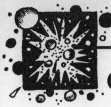

GRAPES, RAISINS, AND KIDNEYS

Drying grapes to make raisins is a way to keep them from spoiling. Water evaporates from the fruit, but the chemicals that give the grapes their sweetness, colour, and flavour are left inside the wrinkled skins. If you soak a handful of raisins in a glass of water for several hours, they become round again and the water turns reddish-brown and tastes sweet. This happens because of two processes called osmosis and dialysis.

Water enters the raisin through very tiny holes in its skin called pores. This movement of water is osmosis. At the same time, sugar molecules inside the raisin come out through its skin and into the water. This movement of chemicals is dialysis. In this example, the sugar molecules are small enough to pass through the skin of the fruit, but the large starch molecules cannot pass through. So dialysis separates these two chemicals. Osmosis and dialysis are important processes in our bodies.

Dialysis occurs in our kidneys through thin sheets of body tissue that remove the small molecules of body wastes from our blood. When kidneys do not work properly and dialysis cannot happen, a person becomes very sick and will die. People like this must go to a hospital every few days to be connected to a dialysis machine. These "artificial kidneys" are made from long tubes of thin plastic. A tube is put into the person's arm or leg, and their blood goes through the machine where it is purified through dialysis. The blood goes back into the person through another tube. This takes several hours.

Orange juice concentrate is made through reverse osmosis. Orange juice is put into a wide tube and pressure is applied. The water moves out of the tube, leaving the concentrate behind. We buy the concentrate, add water, and drink orange juice. Salt water can be desalinated (the salt removed) in the same way. Fresh water comes out through the walls of a tube, but the salt stays behind.

INFORMATION AND MEMORY

Information is stored in our genes and in our brains. Gene information is stored in our body cells as the chemical deoxyribonucleic acid (DNA). We inherit our DNA from our parents. DNA contains everything our bodies need to know to do on their own, like laughing, walking, reproducing, and digesting. It also contains the information that determines what we will be like—our hair colour, whether we'll be right- or left-handed, which parent we might look more like. We are born with DNA in our cells, and as new body cells grow to replace old ones, our DNA and its information is copied into the new cells.

Scientists measure information in bits. A book of 500 pages contains about 15 million bits. We have more than five billion (5,000 million) bits of life information in each of our cells. If you were able to stretch the DNA in one of your cells, it would measure about 2 metres (6 feet). Yet all the DNA in your whole body weighs only about 90 grams (3.2 ounces).

Scientists have learned a lot about DNA, and they continue working to find out more. But they know a lot less about how information is stored and used by the chemicals in our brains. There are about one hundred million million nerve cells in the brain, and there are probably at least that number of bits of stored information. We use some of this information unconsciously to keep our hearts beating and our lungs breathing. We also store information as memories.

You can measure your memory with a solitaire game called Concentration, which you can play with a deck of cards or a computer game. Deal a deck of cards face down, then turn up two cards. If the two cards are a pair, put them aside and turn up two more cards. If the cards are a pair, put them face down and try again. (Try and remember what cards you've looked at.) Your best score is the smallest number of tries it takes you to match all the cards.

Dr. Wilder Penfield, a neurosurgeon at McGill University in Montreal, showed that memories are stored in the brain and can be recalled by touch. When Dr. Penfield touched a part of a patient's brain, the patient heard music that he had heard only once many years ago. Doctors can look at the brains of patients with instruments called scanners. These scanners show what part of the brain is being used when the patient is thinking or listening to music. Scientists know that brain information is chemical in nature, but they do not know how it is stored. This is one of the biggest problems scientists have ever tried to solve.

Appendices

CONTENTS

PERIODIC TABLE OF THE ELEMENTS

The Periodic Table on page 15 includes the names, symbols, atomic numbers, atomic masses, and even the state (solid, liquid, or gas) of each of the chemical elements as they exist at 20°C (68°F). On this page there is a blank copy of the Periodic Table that you may photocopy to test how much you can recall about the different elements or to use to write in the names of the elements that you identified in your room when you made a chemical map of it (page 17).

DISCOVERY OF THE CHEMICAL ELEMENTS

The table below lists the chemical
elements and when each of them
was discovered. How many were
known when you were born? Your
parents? Your grandparents?

Name	Symbol	Atomic Number	Discovered
Actinium	Ac	89	1899
Aluminum	Al	13	1825
Americium	Am	95	1944
Antimony	Sb	51	1450
Argon	Ar	18	1894
Arsenic	As	33	13th C
Astatine	At	85	1940
Barium	Ba	56	1808
Berkelium	Bk	97	1949
Beryllium	Be	4	1798
Bismuth	Bi	83	15th C
Boron	B	5	1808
Bromine	Br	35	1826
Cadmium	Cd	48	1817
Calcium	Ca	20	1808
Californium	Cf	98	1950
Carbon	C	6	B.C.
Cerium	Ce	56	1803
Cesium	Cs	55	1860
Chlorine	Cl	17	1774
Chromium	Cr	24	1797
Cobalt	Co	27	1735
Copper	Cu	29	B.C.
Curium	Cm	96	1944
Dysprosium	Dy	66	1886
Einsteinium	Es	99	1952
Erbium	Er	68	1843
Europium	Eu	63	1901
Fermium	Fm	100	1953
Fluorine	F	9	1771
Francium	Fr	87	1939

Name	Symbol	Atomic Number	Discovered
Gadolinium	Gd	64	1886
Gallium	Ga	31	1875
Germanium	Ge	32	1886
Gold	Au	79	B.C.
Hafnium	Hf	72	1923
Hahnium	Ha	105	1970
Hassium	Hs	108	1984
Helium	He	2	1868
Holmium	Ho	67	1878
Hydrogen	H	1	1766
Indium	In	49	1863
Iodine	I	53	1811
Iridium	Ir	77	1804
Iron	Fe	26	B.C.
Krypton	Kr	36	1898
Lanthanum	La	57	1839
Lawrencium	Lr	103	1961
Lead	Pb	82	B.C.
Lithium	Li	3	1817
Lutetium	Lu	71	1907
Magnesium	Mg	12	1829
Manganese	Mn	25	1774
Meitnerium	Mt	109	1982
Mendelevium	Md	101	1955
Mercury	Hg	80	B.C.
Molybdenum	Mo	42	1782
Neodymium	Nd	60	1885
Neon	Ne	10	1898
Neptunium	Np	93	1940
Nickel	Ni	28	1751
Nielsbohrium	Ns	107	1976
Niobium	Nb	41	1801
Nitrogen	N	7	1772
Nobelium	No	102	1958
Osmium	Os	76	1804
Oxygen	O	8	1774
Palladium	Pd	46	1803
Phosphorus	P	15	1669
Platinum	Pt	78	1735

Name	Symbol	Atomic Number	Discovered
Plutonium	Pu	94	1940
Polonium	Po	84	1898
Potassium	K	19	1807
Praseodymium	Pr	59	1885
Promethium	Pm	61	1945
Protactinium	Pa	91	1917
Radium	Ra	88	1898
Radon	Rn	86	1900
Rhenium	Re	75	1925
Rhodium	Rh	45	1803
Rubidium	Rb	37	1861
Ruthenium	Ru	44	1845
Rutherfordium	Rf	104	1969
Samarium	Sm	62	1879
Scandium	Sc	21	1879
Seaborgium	Sg	106	1974
Selenium	Se	34	1879
Silicon	Si	14	1823
Silver	Ag	47	B.C.
Sodium	Na	11	1807
Strontium	Sr	38	1790
Sulphur	S	16	B.C.
Tantalum	Ta	73	1802
Technetium	Tc	43	1937
Tellurium	Te	52	1782
Terbium	Tb	65	1843
Thallium	Tl	81	1861
Thorium	Th	90	1828
Thulium	Tm	69	1879
Tin	Sn	50	B.C.
Titanium	Ti	22	1791
Tungsten	W	74	1783
Uranium	U	92	1789
Vanadium	V	23	1830
Xenon	Xe	54	1898
Ytterbium	Yb	70	1878
Yttrium	Y	39	1794
Zinc	Zn	30	B.C.
Zirconium	Zr	40	1788

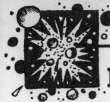

NOBEL PRIZES FOR CHEMISTRY

Alfred Bernhard Nobel lived from 1833 until 1896. He was a Swedish inventor who made a fortune from his invention of dynamite. At his death, he left a fund equivalent to many millions of dollars for the establishment of annual prizes (known as the Nobel Prizes) in five areas: Peace, Literature, Physics, Chemistry, and Physiology and Medicine. These prizes have become the supreme honour that can be won for achievements in each of the above fields. In 1958 a new element was discovered and was named for this famous man. Nobelium (atomic number 102) has the symbol No.

This table contains the names of the Nobel Prize Winners in chemistry up to 1993, where the work was done, and a practical use of their discovery. There is space at the end of this table for you to add future Nobel laureates in chemistry.

Year	Name	Country	Use
1901	Jacobus Henricus Van't Hoff	Holland	Concentrating orange juice
1902	Emil Fischer	Germany	Sugars and proteins in food
1903	Svante August Arrhenius	Sweden	Testing acidity of foods and soil
1904	Sir William Ramsay	Great Britain	Helium balloons and neon signs
1905	Adolf von Baeyer	Germany	Making dyes and drugs
1906	Henri Moissan	France	Making non-stick pots and pans
1907	Eduard Buchner	Germany	Baking and brewing
1908	Ernest Rutherford	Great Britain	Tracing chemicals in the body
1909	Wilhelm Ostwald	Germany	Catalysing chemical change
1910	Otto Wallach	Germany	Making perfumes from plants
1911	Marie Curie	France	Using radium and polonium
1912	Francois A.V. Grignard	France	Making carbon compounds
	Paul Sabatier	France	Making saturated fats
1913	Alfred Werner	Switzerland	Making metal compounds
1914	Theodore W. Richards	United States	Measuring weights of atoms
1915	Richard Willstatter	Germany	Making pigments from plants
1916	(no award)		
1917	(no award)		
1918	Fritz Haber	Germany	Making fertilizer from air
1919	(no award)		
1920	Walther Nernst	Germany	Hurrying chemical reactions
1921	Frederick Soddy	Great Britain	Using heavy and light atoms
1922	Francis W. Aston	Great Britain	Filling the Periodic Table

1923	Fritz Pregl	Austria	Measuring amounts of elements
1924	(no award)		
1925	Richard Zsigmondy	Germany	Making custard, catsup, and paint
1926	Theodor Svedberg	Sweden	Separating protein molecules
1927	Heinrich O. Wieland	Germany	Treating gall bladder disease
1928	Adolf Windaus	Germany	Making vitamins and drugs
1929	Sir Arthur Haden and Hans A.S. von Euler-Chelpin	Great Britain Germany	Baking, brewing, making wine and corn syrup
1930	Hans Fischer	Germany	Measuring crops from space
1931	Karl Bosch and Friderich Bergius	Germany	Making ammonia for fertilizer and liquid coal for fuel
1932	Irving Langmuir	United States	Making artificial cell walls
1933	(no award)		
1934	Harold Clayton Urey	United States	Making heavy water
1935	Frederic and Irene Joliot-Curie	France	Making chemical elements
1936	Peter J.W. Debye	Holland	Measuring gas molecules
1937	Sir Walter N. Haworth	Great Britain	Sugars and vitamin C in food
	Paul Karrer	Switzerland	Vitamins A and B_2 in food
1938	Richard Kuhn (declined)	Germany	Carotenes and vitamins in food
1939	Adolf Butenandt (declined)	Germany	Sex hormones in health
	Leopold Ruzicka	Switzerland	Preventing heart attacks
1940	(no award)		
1941	(no award)		
1942	(no award)		
1943	Georg von Hevesy	Hungary	Tracing atoms in the body
1944	Otto Hahn	Germany	Using atomic energy
1945	Artturi Virtanen	Finland	Storing food and fodder
1946	James B. Sumner	United States	Crystallizing enzymes
	Wendell M. Stanley and John H. Northrup	United States	Preparing pure enzymes and virus proteins for medicine
1947	Sir Robert Robinson	Great Britain	Growing plant chemicals
1948	Arne Tiselius	Sweden	Separating blood proteins
1949	William Francis Giauque	United States	Doing extremely cold chemistry
1950	Otto Diels and Kurt Alder	Germany	Making carbon compounds
1951	Edwin M. McMillan and Glenn T. Seaborg	United States	Making smoke detectors from a synthetic chemical element
1952	Archer J.P. Martin and Richard Synge	Great Britain	Separating mixtures of chemical compounds
1953	Herman Staudinger	Germany	Making chemical fibers
1954	Linus Pauling	United States	Making bonds in molecules
1955	Vincent du Vigneaud	United States	Making synthetic hormones

1956	Sir Cyril Hinshelwood and	Great Britain	Making plastics, flames, and explosions
	Nikolai N. Semenov	Soviet Union	
1957	Lord Todd	Great Britain	Making parts of DNA molecules
1958	Frederick Sanger	Great Britan	Treating diabetes with insulin
1959	Jaroslav Heyrovsky	Czechoslovakia	Measuring dissolved chemicals
1960	Willard F. Libby	United States	Radiocarbon dating of fossils
1961	Melvin Calvin	United States	Growing plants with sunlight
1962	Sir John C. Kendrew and	Great Britain	Photographing protein molecules with x-ray cameras
	Max F. Perutz		
1963	Guilio Natta	Italy	Making polymers and plastics
	Karl Zeigler	Germany	Making metal catalysts and plastics
1964	Dorothy C. Hodgkin	Great Britain	Using vitamin B_{12} and penicillin
1965	Robert B. Woodward	United States	Making vitamin B_{12}
1966	Robert S. Mulliken	United States	Making atoms into molecules
1967	Manfred Eigen	Germany	Measuring rapid chemical reactions
	Ronald G.W. Norrish and	Great Britain	
	George Porter		
1968	Lars Onsager	United States	Measuring energy changes
1969	Derek H.R. Barton	Great Britain	Changing the shapes and reactions of molecules
	Odd Hassel	Norway	
1970	Luis F. Leloir	Argentina	Storing energy in living things
1971	Gerhard Herzberg	Canada	Fingerprinting molecules
1972	Christian B. Anfinsen,	United States	Making and using enzymes
	Stanford Moore, and		
	William H. Stein		
1973	Geoffrey Wilkinson and	Great Britain	Making carbon compounds containing metal atoms
	Ernst Fischer	Germany	
1974	Paul John Flory	United States	Measuring polymer molecules
1975	J.W. Cornforth and	Australia	Mapping the paths of molecules in chemical reactions
	Vladimir Prelog	Switzerland	
1976	William S. Lipscomb, Jr.	United States	Making compounds of boron
1977	Ilya Prigogine	Belgium	Calculating heat in reactions
1978	Peter D. Mitchell	Great Britain	Measuring the energy of cells
1979	Herbert C. Brown and	United States	Making chemical bonds in the manufacture of drugs
	Georg Wittig	Germany	
1980	Paul Berg and Walter Gilbert	United States	Makings parts of DNA molecules
	Frederick Sanger	Great Britain	
1981	Kenichi Fukui and	Japan	Predicting the course of chemical reactions
	Roald Hoffman	United States	
1982	Aaron Klug	South Africa	Electron microscopy of DNA
1983	Henry Taube	United States	Measuring reactions of metals
1984	R. Bruce Merrifield	United States	Making proteins automatically

Year	Name	Country	Description
1985	Herbert A. Hauptman and Jerome Karle	United States	Photographing the molecules of life with x-ray cameras
1986	Dudley R. Herschbach and Yuan T. Lee	United States	Measuring and calculating the pathways of atoms and molecules in chemical reactions
	John Polanyi	Canada	
1987	Jean-Marie Lehn,	France	Making and using artificial molecules that work like natural molecules
	Donald J. Cram, and Charles J. Pedersen	United States	
1988	Hartmut Michel, Johann Deisenhofer, and Robert Huber	Germany	Measuring how green plants use solar energy
1989	Sidney Altman and Thomas R. Cech	United States	Using RNA as a chemical catalyst in living cells
1990	Elias J. Corey	United States	Making natural drugs in the lab
1991	Richard R. Ernst	Switzerland	Seeing atoms in magnetic fields
1992	Rudolph A. Marcus	United States	Calculating reaction pathways
1993	Michael Smith	Canada	Making new genes
	Kary Mullis	United States	DNA fingerprinting
1994			
1995			
1996			
1997			
1998			
1999			
2000			

INDEX

ACKNOWLEDGEMENTS/ABOUT THE AUTHORS

Douglas Hayward and Gordon Bates gratefully acknowledge the hard work and support of many friends and colleagues at the University of British Columbia and elsewhere, and the Vancouver section of the Chemical Institute of Canada for its sustained interest and sponsorship in the "Do-It-Yourself Chemistry" program. They would also like to extend special thanks to Tom Blinkhorn, principal of William Bridge Elementary School in Richmond, B.C., who extended the first invitation to the authors to visit a school with the "Do-It-Yourself Chemistry" program, and to all the principals, teachers, and students who have subsequently welcomed the program into their classrooms. The generous financial assistance provided by the national office and the Vancouver Section of the Chemical Institute of Canada, the Chemical Education Trust Fund of the Chemical Institute of Canada, Science Culture Canada, the British Columbia Science & Technology Development Fund, the Company Associates of the Canadian National Committee of the International Union of Pure and Applied Chemistry, and by the "Scientists and Innovators in the Schools" program of the British Columbia government has helped make the program and the development of this book possible.

Gordon Bates received his PhD in Organic Chemistry from the University of Alberta in 1976, and has taught at the University of British Columbia since 1977. In addition to being one half of the writing team behind *It's Elementary!*, Gordon Bates coordinates fund raising for the Do-It-Yourself Chemistry program through which he and Douglas Hayward introduce thousands of British Columbia school children to the world of chemistry each year.

Douglas Hayward began his teaching career in a one-room country school in Saskatchewan in 1938. He received a PhD in Organic Chemistry from McGill University in 1949, and since then has held faculty appointments at the University of British Columbia and six other universities in Europe and Canada. His research on left and right handed molecules and drugs for treating heart attacks has led to three patents and the publication of over thirty chemical research papers.

Since 1986 Professor Hayward has carried out hands-on chemistry experiments with more than 17,000 students in elementary schools in British Columbia, Canada. He has received the Canadian Patents and Development Limited's Inventors Award and the Eve Savory Award for Science Communication.

NOTES

NOTES

NOTES

NOTES

NOTES